# FIRE UP!
## your employees
### AND SMOKE YOUR COMPETITION!

## HOW TO
## INVITE
## INCITE
## and
## IGNITE
### EMPLOYEE
### PERFORMANCE

## Jay Forte

Author Photo by Howard Zucker.

DISCLAIMER: This publication is designed to provide accurate and
authoritative information in regard to the subject matter covered. It is sold
with the understanding that the publisher and author are not engaged in
rendering legal advice, or any other professional service to the reader. If legal
advice or other expert assistance is required, the services of a competent
professional person should be sought. The reader should take note that laws
and rules applicable to their situation may change. It is the responsibility
of the reader to seek further professional guidance whenever necessary. The
author, publisher, and seller jointly and severally disclaim any warranty,
express or implied, for any general or particular purpose, including any
warranty of merchantability.

ISBN 10: 1-931945-95-0
ISBN 13: 978-1-931945-95-0

Library of Congress Catalog Number: 2009922743

Printed in the United States of America
First Printing: March 2009

13  12  11  10  09     5  4  3  2  1

Expert Publishing, Inc.
14314 Thrush Street NW,
Andover, MN 55304-3330
1-877-755-4966
www.expertpublishinginc.com

To Jeff, Kristin, Karalyn, and Kate,
whose constant energy, love, and support
engages, inspires, and fires me up.

# CONTENTS

*"To be built to last,
you have to be built
for change."*

*Jim Collins*

## A Personal Note from the Author

The goal of this book is to help all organizations grow their bottom lines by maximizing every employee's contribution and performance. As I write this, these same employees are actively disinterested and uninspired in the workplace. Managers continue to dictate and demand employees to perform, using management methods that are ineffective and outdated. These outdated methods divert workplace energy into a battle of wills instead of into a united, collaborative, and results-oriented focus on performance. This workplace battle for results is perpetuated more by ineffective management than by confrontational or lazy employees. Our world has changed but our management methods have not. Intellectual-age employees do not respond to industrial-age management and the shrinking bottom line reflects that most organizations do not know this or know how to change with the times.

Despite the significant number of business books, programs, and resources available, managers and leaders have not yet consistently learned how to connect today's employees to performance. The amount of materials available to management now confuse instead of educate. What is needed is a clear theory of what to do to manage in an intellectual age, and a comprehensive instruction guide to show how to implement this theory today, real time, in our actual workplace. This is the purpose of *Fire Up! Your Employees and Smoke Your Competition.*

As a CFO, corporate educator, speaker, and performance consultant, I have worked with managers and leaders struggling to activate employees to perform and contribute. In virtually every case, the inability of these leaders and managers to achieve their desired results was because their management approach was ineffective with today's employees. This has compelled me to prepare and present not only a clear and concise theory of millennial management (the what), but a practical implementation process (the how) that I call the Fire Up! Process<sup>SM</sup>. To perform today, employees need to be excited, engaged – in short, fired up.

The Fire Up! Process<sup>SM</sup> is based on the three components of INVITE, INCITE, and IGNITE employee performance:

1. INVITE: Millennial managers invite the best by creating an employee-focused culture that supports, respects, appreciates, and attracts employees. They hire employees based on specific talents (not strictly skills and experience) and thinking in order to invite the best talents and people to the organization. This connects employees intellectually to their work.

2. INCITE: Millennial managers incite or activate employees to step up and own their work by creating customized roles around employees' talents, values, and interests, and the needs of the business. They also establish performance expectations that define the standard of performance (the end), but leave the process to achieve them to the employee. Employees now have a voice in how they complete their work; they act and think like owners. This connects employees emotionally to their work.

3. IGNITE: Millennial managers ignite performance by spending meaningful time with each employee through recurring performance feedback and career development. This connection between employee and manager is the key to igniting employee loyalty and performance, and is core to millennial management. This connects employees emotionally to their managers.

The pressure is on you; today's poor performance is more a statement about management than employees. You have the ability to Fire Up! employees – to achieve extraordinary performance – or douse the flames of enthusiasm. Employees come to the workplace looking to make a difference. It is in the relationship with you that this spirit is ignited or extinguished. Employees stay or go because of you. Employees actively commit or do great things or as little as possible because of you. Employees are engaged or actively disengaged because of you. It all comes back to you and how you manage.

I want your organization to have the best employees who impress both you and your customers. I want your organization to have employees who innovatively spot and react to opportunities. I want your employees to act and think like owners, taking personal responsibility for driving performance and results. Only then will your organization be competitive enough to lead in today's roller coaster economy. And as I see it, most organizations are not able to make this happen. They are locked in a battle of wills with their employees and have not learned how to engage and inspire the intellectual-age employee to perform. This book will introduce a Process that will end the battle of wills and direct employee energy into performance.

You will see this is not a conventional business book. It is built on the shared collective perspectives of contemporary authors, thinkers, and business professionals who publicly offer their ideas about management, employees, and performance, coupled with my research and perspectives from years of teaching adult learners, managers, and leaders. All great ideas use other ideas and perspectives as inspiration; this encourages continual progress in understanding our changing world and developing responses that have the greatest impact. However, what is frequently missing in contemporary business authors' work is the guidance and instruction to move from the theory to practice – from ideas to implementation. Our world requires practical solutions. Though it is always a great thing to be able to dialog and discuss theory, at the end of the day we must not only be smarter, but we must also have a plan to be better. This book presents both – theory (the what) and practice (the how) with activities, exercises, and worksheets hosted on the text's supporting website (www.FireUpYourEmployees.com). Its goal is to educate today's managers in the methods to connect employees intellectually and emotionally to the work, the workplace, and their management, resulting in extraordinary performance. Significant bottom-line performance is the goal.

## How to Use This Resource

Since this text presents both theory and a full implementation process, you will need some guidance to use it effectively and to get the greatest impact for your organization. This is my recommendation how to proceed for the greatest results.

## Before You Start This Book

First, to have a clear perspective of the entire Process, review the Fire Up! Process$^{SM}$ Overview on page 11 and the Step-by-Step Process Instructions on page 13. These will not only show you the complete Fire Up! Process$^{SM}$, but they also introduce its terminology and tools to help prepare you to implement the Fire Up! Process$^{SM}$. The theory that supports the Fire Up! Process$^{SM}$ is summarized in this text. Each step of the Process includes the text's corresponding chapter numbers for easy reference.

Once you have reviewed the Process and have a basic understanding of its steps, review the Fire Up! Process$^{SM}$ Summary of Tools on page 21; these tools are available in each chapter's link on the Fire Up! website (www. FireUpYourEmployees.com). The text will direct you when to access the tools to enhance your learning and practice to develop your confidence with the Process.

## Start the Book

As you start each chapter, you will be directed to go to the Fire Up! website (www.FireUpYourEmployees.com). On the website, print the chapter's corresponding worksheets, exercises, and activities and have them ready as you progress through each chapter. The text will guide you when to access these additional pages. You will also be asked to create action items as you progress through each chapter to help you implement the Fire Up! Process$^{SM}$ in your organization. The best way to become successful and confident with this Process is to complete the exercises and activities before advancing to the next chapter. Note that the Fire Up! Process$^{SM}$ is a step-by-step process with worksheets and forms to help you easily, quickly, and comprehensively learn how to connect your employees both emotionally and intellectually to their work and workplace. As a process, practice will be the best way to fully implement its concepts and tools and benefit from its ability to significantly impact performance and results.

Initially, you will first practice with fictitious employees and events. As you progress, you will be asked to involve your actual employees. This will connect the Fire Up! Process$^{SM}$ to your workplace and give you the ability to see its impact with actual employees, in actual workplace situations. Its greatest benefit to you is to see both theory and practice in your workplace.

I believe most employees want to be great; they want to contribute and be noticed for making a difference. I also believe most of today's managers do not know how to help employees be great. They are unfamiliar with the best methods to manage the intellectual-age employee. As a result, performance is average, employee turnover is high and most employees are disengaged. By understanding the theory of the Fire Up! Process$^{SM}$, and developing the practice and proficiency with its components, you will see a dramatic change in your connection with and the engagement levels of your employees. As employee engagement increases, you will see greater contribution, greater responses, and less turnover. Your workplace will start to attract and retain the best employees. They will become more fired up about what they do, and when fired up, they will smoke your competition.

**Jay Forte**

*"Every great idea starts
out as blasphemy."*
Bertrand Russell

# Introduction

## Ignite the Fire for Passionate Performance

*To fire them up, you must know how they spark.*

In extraordinary organizations, all employees are excited and energized, their brains sparking with ideas, inventing solutions, and contributing in all areas. They connect with their jobs; they connect with their managers. These connections fan their performance sparks into an all out fire of passionate performance. Employees actively contribute in ways that use their talents and strengths. Employees voice their opinions, solve problems, and invent opportunities. Employees think and act like owners because they are engaged, passionate, and fired up about what they do.

In average organizations, we occasionally see the sparks of employee performance – a little extra effort here, a little more creativity there. We see only random sparks, not hot enough to start any fire of performance; these employees are unable to significantly impact results. How an organization activates their employees' passion for performance determines whether the organization will be extraordinary or average. What does the extraordinary organization do that the average one does not? Why is it that some organizations consistently engage and ignite employees' passionate performance while others can barely generate a spark of enthusiasm? The answer is more about you, the manager, than the employee. Let's see why.

When you slept last night, the world changed. It moved from manufacturing to service, from industrial to intellectual, from brawn to brain. As author Seth Godin states, "We used to make food (agrarian society), then we made things (industrial age), now we make ideas (service economy)." Our days are no longer involved doing the same repetitive process that was a significant part of manufacturing or the industrial age. Much of manufacturing moved offshore and left us with a service economy. Service is an intellectual and thinking environment – all brains need to be fully engaged, thinking, inventing, and responding to be successful. We used to provide manpower (physical work) in the agrarian age, horsepower in the industrial age, but today we provide brainpower (thinking and innovation). Employees own this brainpower and it is their choice to offer it, or not. This very fact has significantly affected how employees must be managed. To be effective, our management style must always reflect the needs of those we manage – our employees. Managers must now learn to connect intellectually and emotionally with employees in order to ignite their (passion for) performance. This means you, the manager, must become a better communicator, listener, collaborator, nurturer, and relationship builder. These attributes, previously discouraged in the workplace, are now the drivers of performance.

Performance remains our goal; you now see that you can no longer demand or dictate performance. As Dr. Lois Frankel states in her book *See Jane Lead*, "People don't want to be told what to do, when to do it, and how it should be done. Not only do they not want it, they won't allow it." The focus on strong, centralized, military-based command-and-control management actually works against performance in today's intellectual workplace. Today, you must inspire and engage employees to activate their performance. Today you must INVITE, INCITE, and IGNITE employee performance; you do this through the new and more powerful form of management that focuses on the power of connection – intellectual connection of the employee to his/her role and the emotional connection of the employee to his/her work, manager, team, and organization.

Today, each employee must be fired up and thinking about ways to add value, to contribute, build customer rapport, find opportunities, innovate, and in short, make a big difference in both the job and in the organization. Your people are your profits, or your people's thinking, innovation, and passionate responses drive your profits. It is up to you, the manager, to be the spark that ignites each employee's passion for performance. It is up to you to fire up each employee.

Though you want and need great performance from all employees, the Gallup Organization presents research showing approximately 65 percent of employees do just enough at work not to be fired. Seventeen percent don't care if they get fired because they believe they will easily find another job. That leaves approximately only 18 percent of employees committed, engaged, connected, and fired up – trying their best to make a difference in the workplace and with customers. And though the percentages change depending on the study and on the economic conditions, they indicate that not much more than 20 percent of employees are fully engaged (fired up and excited about doing a great job); all others do less than is required for the organization to be successful.

There is very little likelihood of exceptional performance, achieving significant targets, and growing the business unless:

- You identify that employees (what they know and how they perform) are your organization's greatest assets and, therefore, must be continually, wisely, and aggressively invested in.

- Employees feel they work for an organization that is employee-focused in its culture, policies, and workplace brand.

- Employees connect intellectually to their work. Employees are more inspired to perform when their duties and responsibilities match their talents, strengths, and interests.

- Employees connect emotionally to their work by having a voice in determining how to contribute and how to achieve their performance expectations.
- Employees connect emotionally to you, their manager. Having a successful and professional relationship with you will influence the length of time an employee will stay, how productive he/she is, and how fired up he/she will be.

You, as a manager, have the most influential role in creating a dynamic workforce, and it starts with a new and non-conventional way of looking at your employees. Employees are (intellectual-age) assets to invest in; they are no longer (industrial-age) expenses to manage. As such, you need to regularly investigate ways to secure more significant returns from these assets. You do this by understanding how to grow your investment; in this case, by understanding what employees need to be their best and to continually provide it.

The changes in your world now require you to learn how to partner with each employee – much in the same way you must partner with customers to be successful. The Fire Up! Process$^{SM}$ is transformation management thinking. It offers a new approach to developing your employees' talents and human capital. In each section of this book, I support a hands-on and practical method connecting employee intellectually to their work and connecting them emotionally to their work and to you. Connections focus on the humanity of your employees as thinking, feeling, and emotional beings. The more you allow this back into the workplace, the more you will connect to your employees and inspire them to perform.

So, it is you, the manager who can fan, or douse, the flames of performance. How has the role of manager changed in the intellectual age so you have this impact on employees? A reintroduction to the role of a manager and leader is critical at this point in our discussion.

Things to Consider

- From your perspective, what is the role of the manager?
- What is the manager's responsibility to each employee?
- What is the manager's responsibility to the bottom line?

As you move forward in this new thinking, let's review a perspective offered by Marcus Buckingham and Curt Coffman from the Gallup Organization in their book, *First, Break all the Rules*. Basically, they feel leaders are responsible for the vision and the direction of the organization; this includes a continual focus outward, which looks at opportunities, competition, planning, developing new directions to take advantage of, and invents opportunities to increase our value.

Managers, on the other hand, focus inward; they look into each person. Managers look to understand each employee and help him/her achieve his/her best. Successful managers act as a catalyst to create performance by matching employee talents with company goals and creating performance by matching employee talents with customer needs. And they do this by knowing their employees well and understanding some critical information about management. Again, notice that management approach should be based on the needs of the employees (those you manage) rather than on a one-size-fits-all approach based on the way things have always been done.

Leaders use the powerful team inspired by a millennial manager to fully implement the vision. This collaborative approach ensures a vibrant and high-performing employee base, clearly directed and led through a clearly articulated and well understood vision. Though this still remains the minority perspective, I support this interpretation and will use it to show a more effective and performance-based management approach in connecting to employees.

The best way to exhibit this definition of manager is with a reference to the famous Italian sculptor Michelangelo, the creator of exceptional masterpieces, including the *David* and the *Pieta*. Though these are extraordinary, his finest works are actually those that represent more of what he thought to be the role of the sculptor. As the sculptor, he believed he was charged not with creating a sculpture, but rather releasing from the stone what was already in it. Some of his finest works are the statues known as *The Slaves*; these sculpted emotive male forms are aggressively struggling to be released from the stone. This was the sculptor's purpose – to know what is in the stone and release it. This perspective offers similar wisdom for today's managers. Your role as a manager is to help release the talents of your employees, existing inside them. You need to understand them well enough to know what these talents are and to help employees identify them and develop them for their personal and professional success. You do this by connecting them intellectually to their work and emotionally to you, their management, and the organization.

Before you can move on to the process of implementing a new millennial management approach, you need to review one more area presented by Buckingham, Coffman, and the Gallup Organization. For years, the Gallup Organization interviewed managers and their performance to determine what made managers effective or ineffective.

Their results showed that even though all great managers look different and were involved in a variety of businesses, they all shared one common insight. They realize "People don't change that much. Don't try to put in what was left out; try to draw out what was left in…that is hard enough." In short, work with the talents (strengths) that are in place and don't try to fix or focus on employee weaknesses.

People are who they are. They are like the stone – they must be true to their natures. Buckingham and Coffman's guidance reminds managers not to spend time trying to make an employee something he/she isn't or to do things that are not in line with the way he/she thinks. Instead, spend time encouraging the employee to be better at what he/she is already good at. Each job is a thinking (innovating, creating) job in an intellectual economy. It is now more important than ever that you place employees in roles that match the way they think because this creates the greatest opportunity for an employee to feel competent, confident, and to perform at exceptional levels.

Let's see the Marcus Buckingham's phrase "People don't change that much…" from another angle. His perspective also means a job that requires a particular type of thinking cannot be done by an employee who does not naturally possess that thinking. A core strength or talent (based in thinking) can't be changed; we have what we have. You must, therefore, learn to define the thinking needed in your roles (jobs) and locate employees who naturally share that thinking. You set an employee up for failure when you put him/her in a role that does not match his/her natural thinking. And since specific thinking is the key to your connection to customers and performance, the better matched an employee is to his/her role, the more likely strong performance will result. This will be one of the most fundamental changes in management mindset that has resulted from the economy's movement from the industrial age to the intellectual age. Your focus remains performance; the methods to achieve it have changed.

This new perspective is actually very fundamental. It seems obvious that in a thinking economy, the right thing to do is to match an employee's thinking to his/her role and he/she will think better, be more content, and more engaged. Employees are happiest when they feel most competent and capable. Matching their thinking with the thinking in their roles encourages their performance and confidence. Though this makes great sense, today's managements are not connecting to their employees; they continue to use the outdated industrial-age command-and-control management style of dictate, demand, and define instead of the more effective, dynamic, and passionate inspire-and-engage style. Management's focus on performance mandates, hiring any employee for any role, and spending little time developing or encouraging employees are creating a performance crisis. Employees are not the problem – management is. As was mentioned, management style must always be based on the needs of those being managed. Today's management style must focus on connecting to employees, building strong relationships, empowering them, and holding them accountable for performance and results.

To change to a more successful form of management that actively encourages performance and engagement, I introduce the Fire Up! Process$^{SM}$, a step-by-step process to help all managers learn the fundamentals of managing an intellectual-age workforce, by creating a stronger intellectual and emotional connection with their employees. For those managers who developed their style in the industrial age, this focus on emotional connection may appear challenging. But research supports that this emotional connection is the key to loyalty. In the book *Human Sigma*, written by Dr. John H. Fleming and Jim Asplund, the authors show that customers become loyal (not just satisfied) only when an emotional connection is created with a company, product, or brand. From my experience, their results can also be applied to employees. Employees become loyal (engaged, committed, and high-performing) not only when they connect intellectually to their work (it matches their thinking), but when they also have a personal and emotional connection to their manager and workplace. Emotions, feelings, thinking – in short, humanity – matter in today's intellectual workplace. The happier employees are at work, the more engaged they become; this drives performance. This must, therefore, influence how you manage. This must, therefore, influence how you invest in your employees. This, therefore, influences what drives performance. The Fire Up! Process<sup>SM</sup> offers an approach to consistently engage and inspire employee resulting in extraordinary performance.

The pressure is on you. As I said, today's poor performance is more a statement about management than employees. Today, management success is in strong emotional intelligence – strong human relationships and interaction skills. The days of telling employees what to do are over. Today, you must communicate, nurture, listen, collaborate, and connect – you must inspire and engage – if you want to fire up your employees and help them perform. And when they are fired up, they'll smoke your competition.

# Fire Up!<sup>SM</sup> Process Overview
**Humanetrics LLC**

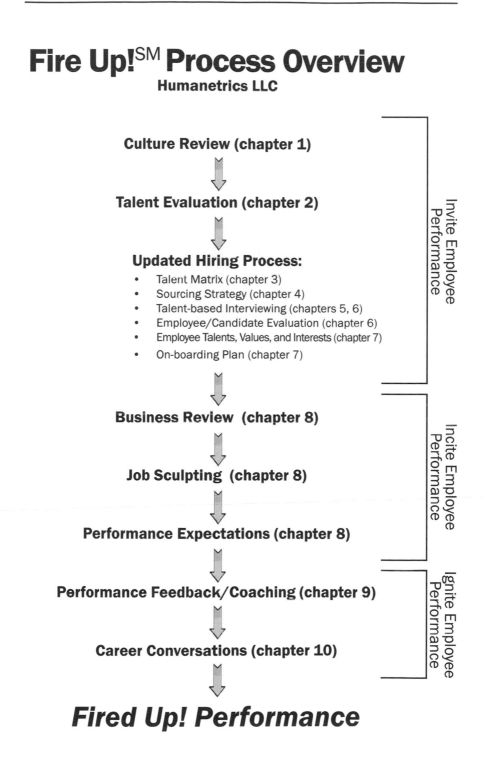

**Culture Review (chapter 1)**

**Talent Evaluation (chapter 2)**

**Updated Hiring Process:**
- Talent Matrix (chapter 3)
- Sourcing Strategy (chapter 4)
- Talent-based Interviewing (chapters 5, 6)
- Employee/Candidate Evaluation (chapter 6)
- Employee Talents, Values, and Interests (chapter 7)
- On-boarding Plan (chapter 7)

**Business Review  (chapter 8)**

**Job Sculpting  (chapter 8)**

**Performance Expectations (chapter 8)**

**Performance Feedback/Coaching (chapter 9)**

**Career Conversations (chapter 10)**

*Invite Employee Performance*

*Incite Employee Performance*

*Ignite Employee Performance*

## *Fired Up! Performance*

# Fire Up! Process<sup>SM</sup> Step-by-Step Instructions

The goal of the Fire Up! Process<sup>SM</sup> is to consistently attract, hire, and retain the best employees. To achieve this, it is critical to understand the millennial management process and to practice with the tools. The more you practice with this Process and worksheets, the more you will connect your employees intellectually to their roles and emotionally to you and their team. All of the worksheets and exercises referred to in these instructions are found on the website: www.FireUpYourEmployees.com, identified by chapter number.

This is the suggested step-by-step Process. See page 21 for the Fire Up! Process<sup>SM</sup> Summary of Tools.

At the end of certain of these steps, you will be directed to add three action items to your action plan. I have included an Action Plan template to accommodate your ideas and action plan items; this Action Plan template will facilitate your success.

**Part 1: Invite Employee Performance: Connect Employees Intellectually to their Roles**

1. Create a powerful employee-focused workplace culture to get noticed and to start attracting the best to your organization (chapter 1). Complete the Ten Components of Employee-Focused Cultures to review the components of a powerful culture; rank those that are most important to your employees, and create an action plan for any changes. With a new focus on culture, consider adding three action items for improvement to this section of your Action Plan.

2. Complete the Talent and Thinking Style Assessment™ (chapter 2). This assessment will define your top four talents and introduce you to a language of talents. Review

the complete list of Fire Up!'s sixteen talents summarized both alphabetically and by quadrant (chapter 2). Develop a working knowledge of talents (terminology and definitions); they are critical for all of the remaining steps of the Fire Up! Process[SM]. Begin to assess which talents will encourage performance in each role in your organization and which are currently present. Develop a plan to define and assess talents. With a new understanding of talents, consider adding three action items for improvement to this section of your Action Plan.

3. Complete the Talent Matrix for one role in your organization (chapter 3). This requires you to identify four (of the sixteen presented) talents that are required to perform this role well. Identify another two (of the sixteen presented) talents that will encourage the new employee to fit well in your organization's culture. Then, list the skills and experience that will help an employee be successful in this role. By learning to complete this form for one role, you will be able to then complete the Talent Matrix for all roles in the organization. This will ensure you clearly define the specific attributes that will make an employee successful and be able to successfully source and hire an employee who will be a good fit for each role. With a new focus on defining the talents, skills, and experience needed in each role, consider adding three action items for improvement to this section of your Action Plan.

4. Use the Role Sourcing Strategy worksheets to create a sourcing strategy for the employee role you identified on the Talent Matrix in step three above (chapter 4). Be sure to focus on the talents required to be successful in the role and to define the locations that you would find others who think in these ways; develop a sourcing strategy to find a candidate for this role. With a new focus on sourcing the right talent, consider adding three action items for improvement to this section of your Action Plan.

5. Review the Humanetrics' Hiring Process to see a successful method to ensure your hiring process is complete and will result in hiring the right employee (chapter 5). Determine which steps you do not currently perform and modify your hiring process to include them. With a new focus on hiring, consider adding three action items for improvement to this section of your Action Plan.

6. Review the General and Specific Talent-Based Interview Questions (chapter 6). Once you have sourced candidates with potential, prepare talent-based interview questions. The powerful talent-based questions have been created around the terms and definitions of the sixteen talent topics listed in chapter 2. For the role you created on the Talent Matrix, locate the specific talents and their corresponding questions. Select several key talent-based interview questions, by talent, from this list as if you were to interview candidates for this role. These questions are designed to evoke the candidate's initial or first response – this is the greatest indicator of talent. Use this as a source of talent-based interview questions that can be customized for your workplace. With a new focus on asking talent-based interview questions, consider adding three action items for improvement to this section of your Action Plan.

7. Once the interview has been completed, you will use the Employee/Candidate Evaluation Matrix to evaluate any candidates for proper fit (chapter 6). Using the talents, skills, and experience listed on the Talent Matrix, empirically evaluate the presence of the attributes noticed in a review of the current employee or of the candidate during the interview. Use the scoring instructions on the worksheet. This will create an empirical and bias-free evaluation process. This will help to identify the best candidate. With a new focus on assessing and evaluating interview candidates, consider adding three action items for improvement to this section of your Action Plan.

8. The Employee Talents, Values, and Interests worksheet is to be completed for existing employees, or for new employees at the time of the job offer, to better understand the employee and to be able to create a powerful customized on-boarding program (chapter 7). Complete this worksheet for the last person hired.

9. Complete the On-boarding Plan – New Employee to ensure the first day/week for a new employee connects the employee to the organization in a powerful way (chapter 7). For the last person hired in your organization, team, or department, complete the On-boarding Plan - New Employee as if the employee were just starting. See what you may have done differently with your new information. Commit to using this worksheet with all new employees. With a new focus on an on-boarding process, consider adding three action items for improvement to this section of your Action Plan.

**Part 2: Incite Employee Performance: Connect Employees Emotionally to their Roles**

10. The key to great employee retention is their inclusion in meaningful and valuable roles that support the organization's critical and strategic organization directions. The Business Review (Strategic Update) worksheets introduce a process to update strategic information to continually assess the needs of the business (chapter 8). This way, as you begin discussions with employees, you will always know the needs of the business and be able to align role responsibilities with the interests, talents, values, and strengths of your employees. Complete this Business Review for your organization, team, or department. Update this monthly or more frequently in periods of great change. With a new focus on regularly updating a strategic understanding of your business, consider adding three action items for improvement to this section of your Action Plan.

11. Complete or update the Employee Talents, Values, and Interests worksheet. This worksheet encourages a get-to-know-you approach between manager and employee (chapter 8). Though this may have been completed at the time the employee was hired or changed roles, be sure to update it on a regular basis (quarterly, semi-annually, or annually) to know any changes affecting the employee. Select an existing employee and complete the worksheet. You will need this information on the employee for the next several steps. Be sure to complete this worksheet on each of your employees at least annually.

12. Complete the Job Sculpting worksheet for the employee you selected in step eleven above (chapter 8). Its purpose is to use what you know about the employee to create a more customized and personalized role that better uses the employee's interests, strengths, and talents. The more customized or sculpted the job is, the more the employee feels emotionally connected to his/her work. Complete this worksheet with the employee. Learn the process and then create sculpted jobs for all employees. With a new focus on job sculpting, consider adding three action items for improvement to this section of your Action Plan.

13. Once you have created a more sculpted role for the employee, work with the employee to complete the Performance Expectations worksheet (chapter 8). These worksheets guide a discussion of the specific performance expectations you have of each employee. It is critical that you define the expectations, but having hired well, leave the process of developing the plan to achieve the expectations to the employee. When employees are given the ability to create their own action plans, they are more activated to performance, and to think and act like owners. Create three performance expectations for the employee you selected in step eleven. Learn the process and create performance expectations for each employee. With a new focus on

performance expectations, consider adding three action items for improvement to this section of your Action Plan.

### Part 3: Ignite Employee Performance: Connect Employees Emotionally to their Managers

14. As often as possible, but at least twice a week, complete the Feedback/Performance Review worksheet for the employee you selected in step eleven (chapter 9). Feedback and performance reviews are a form of educating and coaching; they show employees that you are interested in helping them improve, learn, and become more successful. These worksheets introduce a new and more effective feedback process. Performance is ignited as the relationship between you and the employee grows. A constant performance conversation encourages and activates employees' connection. Learn the process and provide recurring performance feedback for all of your employees. With a new focus on feedback, consider adding three action items for improvement to this section of your Action Plan.

15. The final component that ignites employee performance is career development. Use the Career Conversation worksheets to host a regular career and development discussion (at least annually, though my personal recommendation is that it be hosted twice a year) that looks to match employees' desires for growth and advancement with areas that match their talents and the needs of the business (chapter 10). Employees who have a voice in the creation of their development plan typically become more vested in its implementation. First, update the Business Review (Strategic Update) and the Employee's Talents, Values, and Interests worksheets. Using information from both for the employee you selected in step eleven, prepare the Career Conversations process. You will notice that some sections of the worksheets are completed by you alone, and some are to be completed with the employee.

Develop a career development plan that is implemented by the employee and monitored by you. Learn this process and host it once or twice a year for each employee. With a new focus on the career development, consider adding three action items for improvement to this section of your Action Plan.

These steps create a powerful employee-focused culture, explicit hiring expectations, a new hiring process, powerful on-boarding, job sculpting and performance expectations, performance feedback, and career development. Employees want to be great at work. The Fire Up! Process$^{SM}$ helps them achieve their potential by igniting performance in their talent areas and ensuring they feel valuable and freely contribute. The Fire Up! Process$^{SM}$ is the guide to help all managers become experts at engaging and inspiring employees to achieve their best and to drive great results.

This Process takes commitment, time, and practice to implement. Use this resource, and the tools provided on the supporting website (www.FireUpYourEmployees.com) to practice with this new millennial management concept. As you complete certain of the sections and are confident in their implementation, move from practice to implementation in your workplace. Start slow, solicit feedback, understand the Process, but keep moving ahead. Your employees will respond with performance most managers only can imagine.

# Fire Up! Process<sup>SM</sup> Summary of Tools

This is a summary of the complete set of the Fire Up! Process<sup>SM</sup> tools. Each can be found in the corresponding chapter's on-line materials. Go to the website (www.FireUpYourEmployees.com), click on *Beyond the Book* and select the appropriate chapter to print the supporting tools.

## Part 1: Invite Employee Performance
1. **Attracting employee-focused culture:**
   a. Ten Components of Employee-Focused Culture (chapter 1)
2. **Hiring the right employee:**
   a. Talent and Thinking Style Assessment™ (chapter 2)
   b. Your Primary Quadrant and Four Major Talents (chapter 2)
   c. Talents Review (chapter 2)
   d. Talent Matrix (chapter 3)
   e. Role Sourcing  Strategy Worksheet (chapter 4)
   f. General and Specific Talent-based Interview Questions (chapter 6)
   g. Interview Questions Preparation Worksheet (chapter 6)
   h. Employee/Candidate Assessment Matrix (chapter 6)
   i. Employee Talents, Values, and Interests Worksheet (chapter 7)
   j. On-boarding Plan - New Employee (chapter 7)

## Part 2: Incite Employee Performance
1. **Business issues and opportunities:**
   a. Business Review (Strategic Update) Worksheets (chapter 8)
2. **Connecting employees to their work:**
   a. Job Sculpting Worksheets (chapter 8)
   b. Performance Expectation Worksheet (chapter 8)

## Part 3: Ignite Employee Performance
1. **Connecting employees to their managers:**
   a. Performance Feedback Tool (chapter 9)
   b. Business Review (Strategic Update) Worksheets (chapter 10)
   c. Employee Talents, Values, and Interests Worksheet (chapter 10)
   d. Job Sculpting Worksheets (chapter 10)
   e. Career Conversations Worksheets (chapter 10)

## Creating a Plan
1. **Action Plan Worksheets (Action Plan)**

# Section 1

## INVITE
## Employee
## Performance

*Millennial managers
INVITE performance
when they create strong
employee-focused cultures,
understand talents, and
hire the right employees.
This connects employees
intellectually to their work.*

*"Human capital will go where it is wanted, and it will stay where it is well treated. It cannot be driven… it can only be attracted."*

# Chapter 1

## INVITE the Best
## Create an Employee-Focused
## Workplace Culture

**NOTE** Before starting this chapter, go to www.FireUpYourEmployees.com, click on *Beyond the Book*, and print the supporting exercises and worksheets for chapter 1. This text includes the information you need; the website gives you access to the exercises, worksheets, and activities that will help you more fully complete this chapter and advance your learning through practice.

Organizational culture – it can create a disengaged employee or it can douse the performance passion of an engaged employee. It has the ability to attract great performers or send them running to the competition. It can inspire greatness or encourage mediocrity. It can encourage creative thinking or turn employees into compliant drones. Culture is the least common denominator of all performance and must be addressed as a critical first step of the Fire Up! Process$^{SM}$.

According to author Jerome Want in his book *Corporate Culture: Illuminating the Black Hole*, culture is: "The collective belief systems that people within the organization have about their ability to compete in the marketplace – and how they act on those belief systems to bring value-added services and products to the customer in return for financial reward. Corporate culture is revealed through the attitudes, belief systems, dreams, behaviors, values, rites, and rituals of the company, especially through the conduct and performance of its employees and management."

Organizations can't succeed with an underperforming organizational culture. It is critical to, therefore, define the components of culture, create them, and support them daily. Once in place, they drive the creative, flexible, nimble, and engaging organizational attributes that all employees want to be part of.

Culture is at the very fundamental level of employee ownership. Culture is the spark that activates the employee to use what he/she knows and how he/she feels to perform. The right culture can invite the right employees. In this intellectual economy, it is the employee who determines the quality of his/her work. But it is the quality of the workplace (culture) in attitude and in presence that INVITES the best employees to consider your organization, and once hired, fully contribute and perform. To attract and retain the best employees, your culture must be employee-focused.

When I speak of an employee-focused culture, I speak of the beliefs, attitudes, and policies that concentrate on and celebrate the value of the employee. A more current way to consider this is the employment brand. Employee-focused brands create strong work environments that continually put the employee first – their thinking, their contribution, their inventing, and their performing. Putting the employee first actually allows for the organization to ultimately put the customer first. Employees who work in a powerfully supportive workplace offer their best work and are significantly more engaged. This quality of employee is capable of hearing and implementing a message of extraordinary customer service. Without the supportive and dynamic workplace, the employee is not challenged and not fired up about service or performance.

Performance is really about a fair exchange. You want the best from your employees, and in exchange for that effort, employees want things back from the organization. When an organization knows and provides what employees want and need, employees naturally provide a greater level of commitment and performance. Employees, who do not get the things they want and need from their workplace, are not fired up and, therefore, choose to limit their contributions. So the culture or workplace brand becomes the response to the employee question, "If I do this for you, what will you do for me?"

Think for a minute about a workplace that does not give back to its employees. If the culture components that matter to an employee are missing, the employee starts to search for these components elsewhere. Many organizations have not fully understood the culture components and the power the employment brand has on attracting and keeping (great) employees. The lack of a cohesive and employee-focused workplace brand triggers the great churning of employees who change organizations every eighteen to thirty-six months. This employee movement is due partly to a non-responsive workplace culture and partly to outdated management. The good news is that both can be easily corrected.

When discussing culture, first think foundation and structure. I'll refer to the components of culture as core architecture. Each, on its own, does not create culture; in the aggregate, however, these core architecture components create a workplace brand (culture) that responds to the needs, values, and interests of today's employees. The best way to review culture is through its components.

Review the core architecture components below (adapted and edited from *Performance Consulting* by Dana Gaines Robinson and James C. Robinson). As I develop each core architecture component, think of your current approach and how it may be developed into something more significant. The stronger these core architecture components are, the more they respond to your employees' needs. The more the components respond, the more candidates notice you; this encourages more candidates to apply, which offers you a greater choice to be able to hire the right employee. Once in place, a powerful employee-focused culture retains the best employees because it provides what great employees want and need each day. You will be prompted to access your supporting exercises and worksheets at various points in this discussion of culture and core architecture. To get the full benefit of this approach, complete each exercise before moving on.

### Core Architecture (Culture) Components

Components with a focus on the organization

1. Clearly defined mission (and values), supported by objectives and goals.

2. Clearly defined ethical standards and expectations.

Components with a focus on the employee

3. A competent, talent-based, and bias-free employee selection process.

4. A dynamic on-boarding and inclusionary process.

5. A fair and attainable reward and incentive process.

6. A fair and recurring performance review and feedback process.

7. Regular and recurring skill development (education).

8. Regular and recurring career counseling and development.

9. Dynamic succession planning and mentoring.

10. An inclusive and diverse environment that encourages a free exchange of ideas, employee accountability, and performance ownership.

Components with a focus on the organization

## 1. Clearly defined mission (and values), supported by objectives and goals.

Critical to a strong culture is a clearly defined and pervasively understood mission and values statement; it, therefore, must be a component of core architecture. Employees want to know the mission and values of an organization to determine that the organization has gone through the process to clearly define what it does, why it does it, and what its goals are. This frequently indicates a more stable organization that has well-defined directions and purpose. Once defined, employees can assess whether the mission and goals as presented make sense for whom the employees are and their career directions. Without this information, employees do not know if what they believe, and what the organization believes, are the same or similar enough to create a great working relationship. This uncertainty can lead to performance challenges later in their careers.

In *The Mission Statement Book* by Jeffrey Abrahams, TRINOVA Corporation has the following definition of a mission statement: "A mission statement is an enduring statement of purpose for an organization that identifies the scope of its operations in product and market terms, and reflects its values and priorities." The mission statement is not simply a motto or slogan, but rather a clear statement of the reason for the business that also reflects the personality, ethics, values, and behaviors of the organization. Review the following mission statements, noting that many add their corporate values to their mission statement.

At Microsoft:
- "Our mission and values are to help people and businesses throughout the world realize their full potential."

At Pool Corporation:
- "We provide exceptional value for customers and suppliers, an exceptional return for stockholders, and exceptional opportunities for our employees."

At Cingular:
- "To be the most highly regarded wireless company in the world, with a driving focus around best-in-class sales and service."

At E*Trade:
- "To create long-term shareholder value through superior financial performance driven by the delivery of a diversified range of innovative, customer-focused financial products and services and supported by an operating culture based on the highest levels of teamwork, efficiency, and integrity."

At Caterpillar:
- "Caterpillar will be the leader in providing the best value in machines, engines, and support services for customers dedicated to building the world's infrastructure and developing and transporting its resources.

- Caterpillar people will increase shareholder value by aggressively pursuing growth and profit opportunities that leverage our engineering, manufacturing, distribution, information management, and financial service expertise. We grow profitably.

- Caterpillar will provide its worldwide workforce with an environment that stimulates diversity, innovation, teamwork, continuous learning, and improve and rewards individual performance. We develop and reward people.

- Caterpillar is dedicated to improving the quality of life while sustaining the quality of our earth. We encourage social responsibility."

At American Greeting:
"We create

- Innovative products and services to meet our customers' needs to connect, express, and celebrate.

- Superior value for our retail partners, customers, and shareholders.

- An environment for our associates to excel.

- Collaborative and reliable relationships with suppliers.

- A responsive community presence through leadership and stability."

At Walgreens:

- "We believe in the goods we merchandise, in ourselves, and in our ability to render satisfaction.

- We believe that honest goods can be sold to honest people by honest methods.

- We believe in working, not waiting; in laughing, not weeping; in boosting, not knocking; and in the pleasure of selling our products.

- We believe that we can get what we go after, and that we are not down and out until we have lost faith in ourselves.

- We believe in today and the work we are doing, in tomorrow and the work we hope to do, and in the sure reward the future holds."

At Southwest Airlines:

- "The mission of Southwest Airlines is dedication to the highest quality of Customer Service delivered with a sense of warmth, friendliness, individual pride, and Company Spirit.

- To Our Employees: We are committed to provide our Employees a stable work environment with equal opportunity for learning and personal growth. Creativity and innovation are encouraged for improving the effectiveness of Southwest Airlines. Above all, Employees will be provided the same concern, respect, and caring attitude within the organization that they are expected to share externally with every Southwest Customer."

You can see by these examples of mission and value statements that each reflects the core beliefs and personality of the organization. Though my personal perspective is that most are too long to be easily understood, learned, and lived, they do clearly define the focus and values of each organization. The more clear this statement is, the more the organization can connect to like-minded candidates and employees. The more direct and brief the statement is, the easier it is to learn, live, and support.

As the mission and values are the what of the organization, the objectives and goals are the how. Objectives are more broadly and organizationally designed; goals are narrower and define how strategies will be implemented at a department or other business unit level. It is critical that an organization be explicit about both its identity and its process to process to achieve their identity on a daily basis. This mission clarity encourages a positive employment brand and customer connection since both employees and customers want to know what an organization stands for before they will consider working for or buying from it.

To be effective in hiring the right employee, organizations must have a choice of employment candidates. If the employee culture is not attractive enough to INVITE the best (right) employees, then the organization will be frequently forced to hire those who show up to the interviews instead of hiring employees who are well suited to the roles. A clear mission and values statement clearly defines the organization's beliefs and purpose, which starts to set your organization apart from others. The more clearly you can separate yourself from other organizations, the more your organization will stand out and attract the kind of employees who believe in your mission and values. The more a candidate sees the fit between the person and the organization, the more connected he/she becomes. In a period of workplace uncertainty, low employee skill levels, and retiring older workers, creating ways to attract the attention of your ideal candidates will be critical to your survival.

Things to Consider

- What are your organization's clearly defined objectives and goals that support the implementation of the mission?

- How are the goals and objectives published to the organization?

- How do your employees know their roles and responsibilities in the goals and objectives?

- What input do employees have in the process of achieving the mission or vision?

- How does having a mission statement, supported by goals and objectives INVITE the best candidates?

## 2. Clearly defined ethical standards and expectations.

Success in any organization is based on the standards of behavior and performance that are set both publicly and privately.

Because of the significant number of businesses that have failed or needed outside bailout assistance due to poor decisions or ethical violations (WorldCom, Enron, Lehman Bros, AIG, and others), the ethical perspectives of an organization are now more visible and more openly assessed by applicants and employees. Organizations that openly commit to ethical standards in the treatment of the planet, their employees, their customers, and their compliance to accounting standards and business practices significantly attract applicants from those organizations that do not publicly define their ethical focus. Though organizations are presumed to run their affairs, workplaces, and relationships in an ethical manner, organizations that clearly define their standards, train their employees in the expected behaviors, and act as model citizens significantly attract more ethical employees.

Consider for a minute the focus on green or environmentally-friendly organizations. It is becoming more prevalent for strong employee candidates to do their research to locate organizations that are environmentally-responsible and commit to low carbon impact performance. Ethical responses are now a more significant component of fit used by employees.

This purpose of an ethical statement is much the same as a mission and values statement – to publicly state the ethical standards supported in the organization. This is to ensure that future or potential employees have enough information to know if the organization offers the right environment and fit. Additionally, positive ethical practices actively attract quality employment candidates.

In today's world, success is in customization. We want our food cooked our way; we want our music play lists to reflect our tastes. We want our car to have the options on it that make sense for us, and we want to customize our MySpace site to reflect what we think, like, and believe. Employees want choices and they want to be connected to organizations that reflect their values and interests. Organizations that publicly offer their mission, values, goals, and ethical standards put themselves out to review with the hopes that those prospective employees with like thinking will find them and relate to them. Strong cultures attract those employees who believe what the organizations believe. Without a statement of belief, there is a significant chance that the organization will attract the wrong type of employee and, therefore, negatively affect his/her engagement and performance. Clearly defined organizational perspectives start the process of defining the workplace culture to the rest of the world.

## Things to Consider

- What are your organization's ethical standards statements?

- How are these ethical standards publicized internally and externally?

- What do employees think of the ethical standards and how are these standards lived in the workplace?

- If your organization does not have a statement of ethical standards, what would be involved in its creation?

- How does the creation and publication of ethical standards INVITE the best candidates?

## Components with a focus on the employee

Earlier, I said that the best way to create a customer-focused workplace is to first create an employee-focused workplace. Fired up employees provide consistently extraordinary service – the kind of service that creates loyal customers. Now that I have presented a culture focus on the organization, it is time to move on to a culture focus on the employee. Your focus must be to create a culture that empowers, celebrates, supports, and develops each employee to fire them up. Let's review the employee components of core architecture.

### 3. A competent, talent-based, and bias-free employee selection process.

Employees want to work in organizations that hire for talents and properly match the right employee with the right role. This improves performance, engagement, and competence. An organization that creates a hiring culture that is competent, talent-based, and bias-free, attracts and retains the best employees.

Organizations that commit to hiring employees based on how they think instead of what they look like, the skills they have, or their existing work experience send a message the organization is serious about performance. It commits the effort to invest in its people (treats them like assets, not expenses) by completing significant assessment work up front to ensure the right employee is matched to the right role. Organizations that hire for talent indirectly welcome a diverse workforce. By limiting the hiring decisions to talent fit, organizations disregard gender, age, ethnicity, race, religion, and the other biases that often enter into hiring decisions. Hiring the right talent not only puts the right thinking in the right role, it allows diverse perspectives to enter the workplace because of the great variety of backgrounds accompanying the talents hired in. I will develop this more in the next chapter, but for now, see the impact on candidates and employees when the organization commits the extra work to putting the right employee in the right role. This attracts the best, and once on board, retains the best. Employees want to work in areas that match their talents and strengths and to work with those who are also in their strength areas.

Things to Consider

- What is your organization's current hiring process? How effective is it?

- Is your organization's hiring process based on matching employee talents or using work experience as a reason to hire?

- How will you ensure the business community knows you hire the right employees and give them every opportunity to excel?

- Would your organization's current hiring process INVITE the best candidates to your organization? Why or why not?

## 4. A dynamic on-boarding and inclusionary process.

It is critical for all new employees to be included quickly and completely into the culture of the organization. Studies show that employees who are not actively included in their new organization within their first week consider leaving the organization within their first six months. Imagine having a successful employee selection process – one that takes the time to match employees' talents with their roles – and then does not prepare and support the new employee from the first moment. When asked, employees state that they need to feel part of the organization right from the start to help them feel confident they chose the right organization. Remember, it is critical that both the newly hired employee and the organization believe they have chosen wisely for the employee-organization relationship to be maximized.

Information about organizations that have powerful on-boarding programs is quickly disseminated to the business community. Again, successful hiring practices and an on-boarding program that explain the role's responsibilities, organization's policies, business practices, and introduces the workplace community are all part of the brand of an employee-focused workplace.

On-boarding programs involve the employee from his/her first moment of employment and link the employee personally and professionally with other employees. This link creates an emotional and functional connection so the new employee develops a personal and immediate commitment to the organization. This also helps the employee's connection to his/her role and builds a sense of owner thinking. The on-boarding process will be specifically addressed in chapter 7, as the process is critical in retaining the best employees.

Things to Consider

- What is your organization's on-boarding process?
- What do employees say about this process? If it is not effective, why not?
- Does your organization's on-boarding process have the employee at the center?
- Is your organization's on-boarding process dynamic or "on-boring"?
- How does your organization's on-boarding process INVITE the best candidates?

## 5. A fair and attainable reward and incentive process.

It is critical for employees to see the possibility for reward and incentives as achievable and contingent on their personal performance. It is also fair to have high expectations of employees in today's highly competitive and changing economy; few employees contest the extreme expectations. What they look for is the balance of expectations with rewards. Successful employees are connected to their work and want to be fired up about performance, targets, and goals. However, there are times where extra performance is needed, and in exchange for a strong month-end push on sales or the launching of a new product, employees will look to see that the success of the organization is shared with them. The critical words in this component of the dynamic workplace brand are fair and attainable.

We are in the age of the free agent; employees see that the greatest rewards go to the best performers. So employees who work at extraordinary levels will expect to be applauded and rewarded based on the extreme work. Do the fired up rewards match the performance? If not, employees will commit to less performance. This does not mean the employee is not committed; rather, today's employees see (and demand) more of a connection between performance and pay. All in all, this is actually a great thing for management because employees hold themselves more accountable for performance. To reward the performance, employees will look for the commensurate rewards and incentives that go with the performance. This information is, again, part of an employee-focused workplace brand.

Things to Consider

- What are your organization's reward and incentive programs? Are they effective? Why or why not?

- What do employees know and think about your reward and incentive programs?

- Would your employees assess your organization's reward and incentive programs as fair and attainable or would they assess them as intentionally unachievable?

- How does your reward and incentive program INVITE the best candidates?

### 6. A fair and recurring performance review and feedback process.

It is critical for all employees to be part of a recurring feedback process that regularly discusses all aspects of their performance. Performance done well must be noticed and applauded; performance needing improvement must be corrected. All employees want to know how they are doing. In fact, realize that employees work for more than the money; they work for manager approval. Dialog from a manager about performance is a critical component of all high performing cultures. And for many employees, feedback and praise is the incentive to constantly work harder and improve.

The best way to fire up an employee is to work closely with him/her in areas that he/she is already talented to help him/her become great. Regular feedback, that both applauds success and teaches when performance is not at expectation, is what creates a sound feedback and performance review process. This helps employees who are already good at what they do, become great. Historically, managers have felt the only time they should provide feedback is when an employee is underperforming. In fact, it has been said that many managers believe it is their job to catch employees doing something wrong. If the goal is to create a highly supportive employee-focused culture, then all feedback should applaud successes, and coach and counsel failures with the explicit purpose of helping good performance become great.

Employees should always know how they are doing and performance feedback should not be limited to once a year. It is a great practice, at least annually, to conduct a complete performance review that includes a robust review of employee performance from all areas. However, regular and recurring performance conversations inform employees of performance successes and areas needing improvement. This level of personal and relationship connection – you and the employee – is core to millennial management. The more opportunities you have to provide supportive performance feedback and coaching, the more connected you and the employee become. This fires up the employee to perform at even greater levels and drives personal and professional results.

Things to Consider

- What is your organization's performance review and feedback process?

- What do your employees think about this process?

- Is your organization's feedback process fair, recurring, and have an equal focus on commenting on the good as well as the bad? If not, how can you improve the process?

- How does your performance review and feedback process INVITE the best candidates?

## 7. Regular and recurring skill development (education).

It is critical for all employees to continually learn and to be included in a culture of thinking and high performance. This is the age of intellectual capital; it means employees need to constantly augment what they know to help both themselves and the organization stay competitive. Organizations that commit to regular education and hold employees accountable for using what they learn to drive performance attract the best and retain the best. This creates greater employee loyalty, and in recessionary periods, the organization still performs at strong levels because their employees' base of skills is up to date and competitive.

Today's intellectual-age economy also hosts what is called the emergent worker. The emergent worker is one who takes greater control in advancing his/her career and controlling his/her education. He/she realizes that employees are paid based on their ability to create value for customers and the organization. The more employees know, the greater their value. And the things they need to succeed are now not limited to the technical or hard skills. Today, employees are looking for proficiency with emotional intelligence and soft skills, including communication, relationship building, and collaboration.

We are truly in an idea economy. The best way to encourage idea thinking is to encourage organizational learning and thinking. Employees do not learn unless the learning process is both meaningful and easy to use. Courses should be hosted in areas that directly relate to improving skills and ensuring that employees feel more competent in their roles. Employees should see a direct relationship between what they learn and its application in the workplace. Employees should also be encouraged to continually learn in a variety of areas, including areas that are not in their current role, to determine if they have additional opportunities to contribute. Word gets out very quickly about organizations that help their employees constantly learn, grow, and take on new responsibilities. These are the same organizations that actively involve all levels of management in teaching, sharing what they know, coaching employees in new skill areas, and mentoring employees to accelerate the learning process by blending learning with application.

With the advance of electronic learning (DVD, audio, MP3, and Web seminars), employees have the ability of gathering critical learning in a variety of methods. These new opportunities offer employees flexibility in learning and a method that encourages their personal learning style.

Things to Consider

- What is your organization's focus on learning and is it available to every employee?

- Is it easy for all employees to participate and are topics practical and useful?

- What do employees think about the training and skill development they receive?

- Do employees have the tools they need to be constantly learning and consistently improving?

- How does this INVITE the best candidates?

## 8. Regular and recurring career counseling and development.

It is critical for all employees to be involved in a regular conversation about their professional development and to see that their development process is important to the organization. All employees want to not only know, but also have a voice in determining, where they are headed in their careers. Organizations that host this conversation on a regular basis encourage employees to reach for greater performance in areas that make sense for both the employee and the organization. This encourages greater personal connection between the employee and the management of the organization, which encourages greater employee loyalty.

Notice that I use the term conversation; in this service or intellectual economy, you do not make decisions about employees without employee input. So your discussion about short- and long-term career development must be an interactive dialog or a conversation. In it, the discussions must relate to the short-term role and what is called "job sculpting" – the process of customizing each job around the talents, interests, and values of each employee. This process uses a standard job description as a basis to define tasks and then adds or modifies components to create a more customized role by employees. The goal is to create a more dynamic and more customized fit for each employee so employees come to work excited by what the work allows/needs them to do. This process will be discussed in greater detail in chapters 8 and 10 and will include examples of how to sculpt the ideal job for each employee.

In addition to a conversation about the short term, development also involves a conversation about the long-term role of the employee. Helping employees see the long-term vision encourages employees to commit to the organization, work on skills to achieve the development vision, and see that the employee is valued and respected. Again, all of this encourages employee loyalty. Organizations that host this conversation attract greater candidates since most organizations do not do this and employees want it. As you can see, an organization that commits this time to defining the current role and the conversation (mutual dialog) about the future responds well to what employees want and need from their organization.

Things to Consider

- What is your organization's approach to developing each employee?

- How often is a Career Conversation hosted and what kind of action plan is created?

- What do your employees think about the idea of staying with the organization?

- Are there clear routes for your employees to progress in areas that match their strengths and talents? Is there a plan to keep your employees interested in what they do?

- How do hosting career development discussions INVITE the best candidates?

## 9. Dynamic succession planning and mentoring.

Baby Boomers, seventy-six million born between 1946 and 1964, make up 28 percent of the most skilled workplace roles. The generation behind it, Generation X, hosts only forty-one million, creating an impending supply and talent shortage as the Boomer generation retires. Even if many of the Boomer generation decide to remain in the workplace in a reduced capacity, their departures are a clear and present threat to most organization's workforces, staffing, and intellectual capital. As these senior employees retire, they take with them the knowledge and wisdom of their contributions for the organization. This loss of intellectual capital is the basis for the term "brain drain." Brain drain creates two significant problems: first, there are employment vacancies in the organization if the position is not filled, and second, the replacement employee will not know as much about the role as the retiring party. Both put the organization at a significant competitive risk in an intellectual (service) economy because this economy relies on using what it knows to drive success.

Brain drain can happen as every generation matures, starts to retire, and leaves a younger generation in charge. Organizations can fight the dangers of brain drain by creating succession planning programs. In succession planning programs, employees are selected, trained, and matched with more senior employees to quickly advance not only what they know, but more importantly, how to use what they know. Matching these younger employees with more senior employees through mentoring programs facilitates the process of passing on what the more senior employees know and helps the younger employees to be ready to take over when retirements or departures start.

Having a strong succession planning process tells an employee the organization is thinking and planning for the advancement of its employees, is aware of the retirement process, and is proactive to ensure the organization survives and remains competitive. An organization without a robust succession planning process will quickly lose its competitive edge as those with the knowledge retire or move on. Today's success in business is in what employees (young and old) know. Wisdom (how to use what you know) is built from years of decision-making and is more frequently resident in older employees because of the time and experience in their roles. The goal is to pass this wisdom on to younger employees who may have the knowledge but lack the time and experience (wisdom) to know how to use it effectively. Succession planning ensures that what is important is passed on and that a supply of future management is always being trained to take over and to keep the organization's intellectual capital safe and useful on a daily basis.

Organizations that have a publicized succession planning mindset help current and future employees feel confident the organization will remain, will be competitive, and employees have the room and the direction to grow.

Things to Consider

- What is your organization's succession planning process?

- How are younger employees selected to advance to more senior roles?

- Is there a sense of urgency in the advancement? If not, should there be?

- How does a succession planning process INVITE the best candidates?

## 10. An inclusive and diverse environment that encourages a free exchange of ideas, employee accountability, and performance ownership.

Employees' greatest millennial value is in their intellectual capital – their thinking. This thinking comes in the form of men and women, old and young, varied nationalities, and many religions; this thinking comes in the great diversity of today's workplace. The performance power of current employees is in their combined talents, diverse backgrounds, and a collaborative approach. The more variety in ethnicity, age, gender, and backgrounds, the greater experiences are brought to discussions, projects, products, and teams. This diversity creates great opportunity for non-standard responses, which are consistently proven to be the source of organizational success.

Historically, companies are guilty of "homosocial reproduction." This phrase, coined by Dr. Robert Rodriguez, an assistant dean at Kaplan University, refers to the predisposition of organizations to hire, associate, and work with those who are like them. Organizations that hire employees based on experiences or because of a look or image, miss out on a key component of a thinking and innovating workplace. Homosocial reproduction ensures that employees constantly see the world the same way; the organization clones itself. In the process, it suffers from stale ideas and standard thinking.

Organizations that hire based on talent (not homosocial reproduction) allow for great diversity; these benefit the organization with their histories and colorful traditions that encourage greater innovation, connection, and creativity. Diversity is a bottom line issue and organizations that allow and encourage it consistently outperform those who require their workforce continue to look and act as it always has.

Organizations that support homosocial reproduction also historically are known to tell employees what to do and do not actively encourage or allow employees to freely think, invent, offer ideas, develop new approaches, or try things that are different or unusual. The more management thinks for employees, the more the employees become "idiots" – accustomed to letting management do all of the thinking. Soon, management finds itself handing more and more of the employees' responsibilities. Employees become bored and leave.

Organizations should demand thinking, innovation, and creative suggestions from all of its employees. Employees see and hear things; they have perspectives and they have talents and ideas. Each time you exclude an employee from contributing, you help him/her believe that his/her contributions are not required, accepted, or necessary. Each time this happens, the employee contributes a little less until one day he/she feels there is no reason to stay, or you, as the manager, look at how little he/she is contributing and ask him/her to leave.

Employee-focused cultures allow for employee contribution and participation in all areas. These cultures solicit ideas from every employee and hold employees accountable for generating ideas and problem-solving. Employee thinking is what you pay for when you pay employees; you pay for their ability to think through the best response at each moment of their day. The more the culture expects and encourages employees to contribute, the more they connect to their roles and to the organization. This encourages loyalty and owner thinking.

Organizations that are known to be diverse, open, inventive, creative, and expressive are talent magnets. Employees want to be fired up about their roles; they want to make a significant difference. The outdated command-and-control approach to managing defines employees' contributions and allows very little innovation, spontaneity, and creativity. This process of dictating and demanding alienates employees because they don't like to be told what to do or what to think. Organizations that encourage employee contribution in all areas of the business get noticed. Organizations that encourage ideas and information movement, employee accountability, and full performance ownership INVITE high performing employees because this is the type of culture the high performer wants to work in.

## Things to Consider

- How diverse is your organization?

- Does the organization value diverse backgrounds, experience, and culture?

- How well does your organization include all employees in decision-making, information sharing, and idea solicitation?

- What level of thinking do you expect from your employees?

- What level of thinking do your employees know you expect of them?

- How can an inclusive and diverse environment help to INVITE the best candidates?

Core architecture represents the components of a successful employee-focused organizational culture, or think of it as the Fire Up! workplace brand that attracts and retains the best employees. Employees want to work in a workplace that celebrates who they are and allows them to be great at what they do. Employees want to be treated fairly, given the opportunity to excel, see a long-term path, and asked what they think. Employees want to be passionate and fired up about what they do and how they make a difference. And when they find this level of energy and focus in the workplace, they step up and stand out; they invent the best responses each day for customers, products, policies, and events.

A fired up employee is the key to performance success and results in every organization. These employees control their intellectual capital; they control how hard they work, how committed they are, and how long they stay. Your role as management is to understand this and offer back to them a powerful culture that supports, appreciates, and inspires them to be their best. This type of organization will attract the best candidates for future roles and retain quality employees as the employment market tightens.

Culture is the most fundamental level of performance, as it is capable of attracting the best and retaining the best. Now that you have seen the components that employees (when polled) stated they want and need to see in the workplace, how well do you respond? Does your response provide an indication why the best or the average applicants apply to your organization? Moreover, do the great employees stay with your organization? I will review core architecture components in greater detail as I share more of the INVITE component and introduce INCITE and IGNITE.

Time for Practice

From the worksheets you printed for this chapter from the website, access the worksheet that lists the ten components of core architecture (culture). This exercise will ask you to rank these ten components from your employees' perspective. Once ranked, select the top four components and assess what you currently do and what you could do to make the component more inviting. Create your action plan for this chapter. Remember, as you achieve each of your culture action items, replace it with another to continually improve your employee-focused culture.

## Fan the embers – A summary and review

1.  Core architecture refers to the ten components of workplace culture.

2.  The first two components of culture refer to the organization and to its guiding mission, values, goals, objectives, and ethics. These two components must be in place before all other components can be implemented.

3.  The third through the tenth components of culture are employee-focused. These are things that are done in the organization that continually celebrate, appreciate, and focus on the value of the employee.

4.  Each component may have a different value for your workforce. The goal is to consistently work on all components, starting with the components that are most in demand by your organization.

5.  It is important to always work on developing or enhancing the culture of the organization. Include employees in the discussion to be sure the workplace and culture continually respond to employee needs, values, and issues.

6.  All progress on performance expectations should be summarized regularly; successes must be applauded and poor performance must be coached and counseled. Regular feedback is critical for all successful implementation of performance expectations.

7.  Whatever combination of these ten components of culture you create becomes your employment brand. Is your current brand (word on the street) the brand you want? If not, develop your plan to make the required changes.

*"Man is only truly great when he acts from his passions."*

*Benjamin Disraeli*

# Chapter 2

## How You Spark
## Understand the Role of Talents and Strengths in Performance

**NOTE** Before starting this chapter, go to www.FireUpYourEmployees.com, click on *Beyond the Book*, and print the supporting exercises and worksheets for chapter 2. This text includes the information you need; the website gives you access to the exercises, worksheets, and activities that will help you more fully complete this chapter and advance your learning through practice.

In chapter 1, I focused on the least common denominator of all performance – a powerful employee-focused culture. Organizations with strong cultures that are employee-focused INVITE the best candidates. Once those great candidates are hired into a strong employee-focused culture, they remain longer, contribute more dynamically, and perform more successfully.

The power of a positive culture cannot be underestimated in today's intellectual workplace. Since we need employees to volunteer their effort and participation, our policies and procedures (culture) must make them want to perform at their best. If the policies exist but are not followed, then great employees do not stay. And when they leave (because of the pervasiveness of the social networks that exist – Facebook, MySpace, LinkedIn), comments about your workplace brand make it through the ether at the speed of the click. Because of this connective power, you must work to ensure the workplace brand that is transmitted across the airwaves and ether is positive and correctly highlights the employee-focused atmosphere the organization lives by.

The greatest success of a powerful employee-based culture is the ability to create a supply of quality candidates for your organization. This enables your organization to use a sound hiring process that looks to hire the right employees based on proper fit and talents. Without a powerful culture, the number of candidates (potential employees who would consider working with you) is significantly reduced, making the process of selecting the right employee more difficult. As you will see, it is critical to hire the right employee in the right role. The right employee will be critical to success in an intellectual age.

People have talents; these talents are the natural "sparking" or thinking (otherwise known as the intrinsic abilities) of an employee. All of us have a unique combination of talents; no two of us are exactly alike. Talents are derived in the unique combination of brain connections that evolved early in our physiological development. Talents are innate, and as such, they will always be the source of our greatest performance.

Talents direct the way we think and act; we have no specific control over them. We can't learn a talent because it is already part of our hardwiring – the way our unique brain processes information. Though we can't create talents, (based on your belief system, attribute it to either divine inspiration or genetic evolution), we can develop these natural strengths. This is why I stated we must "hire for talent" (core to who we are – it is just how we think) and "train for skill" (skills can be learned – more on this shortly). But, as is well presented by work done by the Gallup Organization with Marcus Buckingham and Curt Coffman in their book, *First Break All the Rules*, we can only maximize what exists; we cannot add what does not exist and do it well. Or another way to say it is, if something is not our talent area, the best we may become is good.

To be successful today, you must be able to become great – and that can only happen when you use, develop, and focus on your strengths and talents. As you can see, you will need to fully understand the talents that exist in a team, and the talents that are required in each role, for the team and the employee to be successful. Any missing critical talents will affect performance and must be considered in the future hiring process.

As Marcus Buckingham and Donald Clifton say in their book, *Now, Discover Your Strengths*, "If you want to reveal your talents, monitor your spontaneous, top-of-mind reactions to situations you encounter. These top-of-mind reactions provide the best trace of your talents; they reveal the locations of strong mental connections." Talents are intrinsic to us; they are the way we respond and view the world, so unless we stop and think about them, they frequently go undetected or unnoticed. Many times we will actually learn more about our talents from the comments of others, by an evaluation, or assessment.

Studies have shown that in the course of a day, we make twenty thousand three-second decisions. Each of these decisions happens using in our spontaneous, top-of-mind reactions. As such, when we are hired into roles that match our thinking with the thinking required by the role, then most of our twenty thousand three-second decisions will be effective. The more we choose well, the more competent we feel, and the more we are noticed for performing well.

The reverse is true. When we are poorly hired (placed in the wrong role), then most of our twenty thousand three-second decision are not correct. The role needs us to think in a particular way – and we don't think in that way. We do not feel capable or competent. We also strain the employee/manager relationship, as our manager will be consistently disappointed or unimpressed with our performance. The only way to ensure we maximize performance is to first understand that talents drive performance and talents are intrinsic to our thinking. This is why it is critical to hire for talent.

Here is an example: Let's say I am working in a retail store and my natural talents are more social (I like people) than analytical or empirical (I like details). When a customer comes into the store, I naturally go and greet the customers (it is a top-of-mind reaction – one of the twenty thousand three-second responses). I don't formally think about it; I just respond. And since the goal is to connect to customers, I am perceived as social, personable, and friendly. It seems this is a reasonable job for the way I "spark."

Now, let's say I am working in the retail store, but my natural talents are more analytical than social. I am busy reviewing a merchandizing report behind the register when a customer comes in. I look up and look right back down at my work (it is a top-of-mind reaction – one of the twenty thousand three-second responses). It is not because I am mean, callous, or disinterested – it is because it doesn't occur to me to leave my work (analyst) and become social; I don't "spark" that way.

The result of casting an employee into the wrong role is the employee now consistently chooses poorly in the responses to the job. This aggravates both the manager and the customer and the critical fault is that an employee who thinks in one way was cast into a role that requires thinking in a very different way. And, as others will state, the general result of this miscasting of employees is that employee becomes disappointed with the job and leaves or the manager because upset with his/her performance and fires him/her. The problem is the employee thinks in one way, and the role requires thinking in another. I will develop this in the next several chapters. This focus on intrinsic strengths (talents) is core to the Fire Up! Process[SM] approach to extraordinary employee performance.

Talents are also revealed by passionate interest or yearnings – things you love to do. Again from Buckingham and Clifton, "Our strongest [brain] connections [or "sparkings"] are irresistible. They exert a magnetic influence, drawing you back time and again. You feel their pull, so you yearn." Yearning for precision in the role of an accountant is a powerful force and a force equal to the yearnings to be social by a salesman. Both actively pull those who have these talents. Imagine how each would feel if their roles were reversed. There would be no pull; there would be no yearning and ultimately this disconnection would affect performance. In today's intellectual and innovative workplace, it is important employees love what they do. The more connected they are to what they do, the more they are in their talent areas and the better they perform.

Another way to detect a talent is by rapid learning. When you have the ability of learning something quickly or understanding it naturally, you generally have located a talent. It may be an employee who can speak publicly with little coaching or training. It may be an employee who has a natural ability to negotiate successfully and read customer body language without any formal training. Notice how many times you can read the first paragraph of something written about one of your talent areas and already know the content of the remainder of the article. The thinking is natural to you; you get it without being told. Talented people seem to just know because it is natural to the way they think.

A final way to detect a talent is to look at the things that satisfy you. Since talents are based on the strongest brain connections, when you are involved in doing something that matches these connections, you feel satisfied and competent. You enjoy them;

you find time for them. These activities affect your motivation level and your attitude. The greater the level of satisfaction you have, the stronger the talent you possess.

These definitions of talents tell you one more very important thing. Because you now know that talents are the top-of-mind events, the first responses that candidates provide in interviews (when asked new talent-based questions) will offer the best information as to whether a required talent exists or not. This will be critical to your ability to INVITE the best employees.

As you can see, talents are fundamental to all performance. Each of us has specific talents, which means not all employees are a good fit for all jobs. Because we are now in a service or intellectual workplace, success is in the way we think and ultimately invent responses in our work. In the past, it was not as critical to properly match an employee to a job – in the industrial age, there was less independent and customer thinking required of all employees. The workplace was built more on recurring rote procedures that could be learned through training and practice. Today, each employee must think through individual service situations as they occur; very few encounters are the same. That means each employee must be actively thinking and engaged in order to assess and respond in a way that connects each customer to the organization. To be actively thinking and engaged, the employee must like the role, feel intellectually connected to it, and be capable of making the right decisions in the role the greatest amount of time. If not, the employee disengages, service suffers, and the business is negatively affected. All performance success starts with understanding talents.

## A Lesson in Physiology and Development

To better understand that you, as the manager, have no control over the talents of your employees (which is the reason to understand the talents or thinking that each of our roles requires and then work to hire people who naturally have this required thinking), let's review briefly how brains develop. My goal is to show you that your talents are a product of your development and that, as such, you get what you get. Your goal is to understand your talents to learn how to maximize them, not to determine how to change them. For the paraphrased review that follows, I use the guidance and perspectives found in *First Break All the Rules* by Marcus Buckingham and Curt Coffman:

At forty-two days after conception, your brain goes through an explosion of growth. This growth continues for approximately one hundred twenty days at which time your brain creates nearly one hundred billion neurons or brain cells. Starting from approximately sixty days before you are born, these neurons start to make connections with other neurons. These connections or synapses create threads (axons) that link the neurons together; each neuron creates nearly fifteen thousand connections that happen from sixty days before birth to approximately three years old. This is the period where the brain is absorbing all that it can about the world, but with so many connections being made, the brain has minimal ability to create great context or understanding of these connections. So with the complexity and wisdom of life, between the ages of three and sixteen, the weaker synaptic connections start to wither until you are left with approximately half of the original connections. If the brain did not allow some of these connections to wither, you would remain as a child in sensory overload.

Again, from Buckingham and Clifton, "We would never forget – past and present events and would be drowned in particulars, unable to form ideas or to think. We would be unable to feel, build relationships, or make decisions of any kind. We would lack personality, preference, judgment, and passion." The brain is actually more effective with fewer strong connections than with more weak connections.

What remains, once the weaker connections wither, is a pattern of responses that are unique to each of us; no other person has your combination of recurring pattern responses or mental pathways. These mental pathways create your regular and non-intellectual response to the stimuli you receive at every moment during the day. These stimuli (I stated that studies identify them as approximately twenty thousand in a day) are reviewed and assessed by your mental framework. Though you have the ability to stop and formally think in many cases, the greatest portion of your responses will be automatic; these will be done based on the way you are hardwired, and how you process information about your world. This is why some people can do math easily in their heads and others cannot. This is why some people can handle many things at once and others can only handle one or two things at a time. This is why some people are assertive and others are timid. Each of us has a unique set of connections that create who we are, how we think, and what we do. These stronger connections, the ones that remain, create our personality, strengths, passions, and talents.

This discussion of connections also shows your thinking is natural to you and you must be matched to the thinking in your role to contribute your best performance. This concept is core to the Fire Up! Process$^{SM}$ where your focus as a manager is to get to know employees well enough to know how to connect them to the right roles. Remember back to the story of Michelangelo and his sculptor role of knowing the stone to know how to release what was in it. Now that you know this, consider the effect of putting the accountant in the salesman's role or vice versa. Each of them "spark" in a particular way and for them to be effective, their role must allow them to use the way they "spark." Managers who consistently hire employees into roles that do not use their talents, unintentionally disengage employees, and negatively affect performance.

To move on, we must be able to assess the talents or thinking styles of our employees. In today's intellectual workplace, all employees' performance approach can be summarized in the combination of items below:

1.  A thinking (rational more than emotional decision-making) approach to performance,

*Or*

2.  A feeling (emotional more than rational decision-making) approach to performance.

*And*

3.  A directing (self-oriented) approach to performance,

*Or*

4.  A supporting (working through others) approach to performance.

Most people possess a blend of 1 or 2, and 3 or 4, which becomes evident in their talents. To be great in some roles requires a rational approach and more thinking; other roles rely more on feelings and emotions. To be great in some roles requires a more directing approach; other roles require a more supporting and engaging approach to achieve performance. These four attributes will form my Talents and Thinking Style grid to help define core thinking and, ultimately, talents (see Figure 1).

Additionally, it can be said that since talents represent our intrinsic thinking, and our personality and communication styles are also intrinsic to the way we think and process information, then there must be a direct correlation between our talents and our personalities/communication styles. You will see that each quadrant of the Talents and Thinking Style grid will represent core thinking, personality, and communication style. This will be used as the basis from which to define the sixteen core performance talents that are a critical component of the Fire Up! Process[SM].

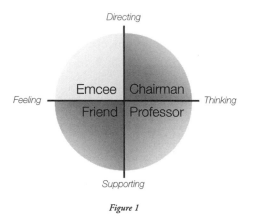

*Figure 1*

Refer again to Figure 1. The initial grid is created by a horizontal axis indicating performance through thinking (rational) on the right and through feelings (emotional) on the left. To that is added a vertical axis that represents performance through a directing approach on the top, and a supporting or engaging approach to performance on the bottom. This creates four distinct quadrants that represent core thinking, behavior, and communication style. As such, each quadrant has been named to identify the core personality of that quadrant, Emcee, Chairman, Professor, and Friend. Each will be reviewed in greater detail as I also introduce the four corresponding talents that define each quadrant's perspective on performance.

Consider this. Each of us has two intrinsic performance drivers – either we approach performance using our heads (in a rational and structured way – thinking) or using our hearts (in an emotional and less structured way – feelings), and we approach performance by directing ourselves and others, or by supporting and engaging others. This combination will now generate sixteen distinct talents, four in each quadrant. This will define the sixteen core performance talents. The clearer you can define the talents needed in each role, the greater opportunity you will have of sourcing and hiring the right employee.

As I introduce the talents by quadrant, refer to Figure 2. The top right quadrant, indicated by the label Chairman, represents the dominant thinking and directing employee. In this quadrant, I introduce the talents of Leader, Driver, Connector, and Bottom-liner. These employees are known for their ability to move quickly, decisively, and with purpose. Their perfor-mance happens in a rational and thinking approach, quick deci-sion-making, comfort in taking charge, and in a personal focus on driving results. This is an empirical results-oriented quadrant, where performance is

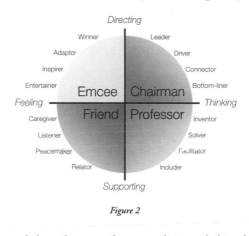

*Figure 2*

measured and empirical, and the talents and personalities exhibited in this quadrant take responsibility for actions, performance, and results. Roles that are well matched to talents that are exhibited in the Chairman quadrant include all roles of leadership, industrial age management, politician, law enforcement, facilities managers, entrepreneurs, administrators, and other take-charge roles.

Employees who test strongly in this quadrant are also intrinsically strong, direct, and assertive communicators; they do not avoid confrontation. They appreciate brevity in details and exhibit a language that is more performance than emotionally-based.

They move and speak quickly, have more formal body language (handshake instead of hug), base responses and actions on fact (thinking), and are more independent and self-reliant.

Employees in this quadrant exhibit performance behaviors inspired by a more thinking approach on one extreme and a more directing approach on the other, though always a blend of the two attributes. The talents represented by this quadrant are presented in Figure 2 and are:

- Leader – Ability to envision and articulate the future; takes control; able to connect actions to results; strategic thinker; unites, directs, and leads others; intellectual, logical, and focused. Quadrant: Chairman – Directing/Thinking.

- Driver – Focuses on doing and getting things done; acts with purpose and direction; establishes order; processes many variables concurrently; organizes and delegates; competitive and focused. Quadrant: Chairman – Directing/Thinking.

- Connector – Problem-solving and systemic fact-based focus; connects facts and performance; defines, performs, and lives by goals and objectives; focused and empirical; methodical, logical, and careful. Quadrant: Chairman – Thinking/Directing.

- Bottom-liner – Focuses on significant performance – exponential instead of incremental; acts with intent; productive and disciplined; thinks carefully and strategically; always results-oriented. Quadrant: Chairman – Thinking/Directing.

Leader and Driver are more defined by their directing than thinking; Connector and Bottom-liner are more defined by their thinking than by their directing and achieving. All four represent the thinking, empirical, directing, and more solo approach to performance, though each highlights a very particular aspect of these attributes.

The bottom right quadrant, indicated by the label Professor, represents the dominant thinking and supporting (working with others) employee. In this quadrant, I introduce the talents of Inventor, Solver, Facilitator, and Includer. Employees in this quadrant are inventive, though pragmatic and focused on details. They are natural learners, teachers and advance performance by working in a thoughtful way with others. Performance is accomplished through their focus on details, guiding and supporting others, and clearly defining and holding a standard of excellence. This is an inventive and relationship-oriented quadrant, where performance is based on thinking, learning, and achieving with, and through, others. Roles that are well matched to talents that are exhibited in the Professor quadrant include educators, instructors, intellectual-age managers, engineers, architects, scientists, accountants, IT, journalists, bloggers, and others who focus on details, analysis, and shared information.

Employees who test strongly in this quadrant are logical, detail-oriented, though indirect communicators; they are openly aware of the feelings, perspectives, and attitudes of others. They exhibit supportive and encouraging language; they ask more than tell. They can be readily identified for their language of, and preoccupation with details, precision, organization, and completeness. The exhibit a more formal body language and more distance in proximity (handshake, greater distance with personal space). Relationships are important for employees in the Professor quadrant and they use these relationships to share and use what they know more than to connect emotionally with others.

Employees in this quadrant exhibit performance behaviors inspired by a more thinking approach on one extreme and a more supporting and working-with-others approach on the other, though always a blend of the two attributes. The talents represented by this quadrant are presented in Figure 2 and are:

- Inventor – Independent, creative, and an on-demand thinker; comfortable inventing, imagining, and innovating; considers the non-conventional; easily sees potential, options, and opportunities; interested in new ideas. Quadrant: Professor – Thinking/Supporting.

- Solver – Approaches performance and relationships logically; methodical and analytical; addresses performance through fact and information; advances skills to be productive; disciplined approach to work and life; perfectionist mentality. Quadrant: Professor – Thinking/Supporting.

- Facilitator – Focuses on learning and teaching others; shares information; advances performance of self and others; detail-oriented; interested in opinions, discussions, and new information; practical thinker. Quadrant: Professor – Supporting/Thinking.

- Includer – Focuses on belonging, contributing, and being part of something important; looks to be understood and appreciated for work and effort; feels connected and helps others feel connected; makes a difference; shares and creates personal contacts; approachable, receptive, sensitive, and loyal. Quadrant: Professor – Supporting/Thinking.

Inventor and Solver are more defined by their thinking than their supporting, relationship-oriented perspective; Facilitator and Includer are more defined by their supporting, relationship-oriented perspective than their thinking. All four represent a thinking and more supportive team and relationship approach to performance, though each highlights a very particular aspect of these attributes.

The bottom left quadrant, indicated by the caption Friend, represents the dominant emotional decision-makers and supporting (relationship-oriented) employee. In this quadrant, I introduce the talents of Relator, Peacemaker, Listener, and Caregiver. Employees in this quadrant are caring, sensitive, and connected to others. They are natural relationship builders, read and understand others well, and are intrinsically good listeners and communicators. Their decisions are made many times by intuition; they are comfortable with emotions and feelings in the workplace. Roles that are well matched to talents that are exhibited in the Friend quadrant include service, retail, health care, mentoring, human resources, teachers (elementary), and support roles.

Employees who test strongly in this quadrant are thoughtful, caring, and empathic. As indirect communicators, they are openly aware of, and receptive to, the feelings, thoughts, and emotions of others. They regularly use supportive and encouraging language; they ask more than tell. They can be readily identified by their language of feelings and emotions, a more informal and close proximity body language (hug, touch), and a more reserved, kind, and quiet demeanor. They develop strong relationships and use these relationships to perform.

Employees in this quadrant exhibit performance behaviors inspired by building supportive relationships, to those who are more inclined to make intuitive or emotional decisions, though always a blend of the two attributes. The talents represented by this quadrant are presented in Figure 2 and are:

- Relator – Builds relationships and personal contact; cares about the feelings, lives, and facts of others; enjoys meeting new people and sharing personal experiences; appreciates uniqueness and diversity of people; relaxed, accepting, and supportive. Quadrant: Friend – Supporting/Feeling.

- Peacemaker – Gets along with others; avoids confrontation; appreciates feelings, emotions, and differences in people; looks to bring and keep people together; looks for commonalities and agreement; value is in personal contact and relationships; open, kind, and genuine. Quadrant: Friend – Supporting/Feeling.

- Listener – Communicates clearly and effectively; takes great care to understand and to be understood; understands emotions and feelings; values personal interactions; patient, tolerant, and non-judgmental. Quadrant: Friend – Feeling/Supporting.

- Caregiver – Focuses on emotions and feelings; aware of feelings in self and in others; selfless in service; appreciates and understands individuality; strong sense of belonging, family, and team; openly cares for and supports others; considerate, empathetic, caring, and compassionate. Quadrant: Friend – Feeling/Supporting.

Relator and Peacemaker are more defined by their supporting, relationship-oriented perspective; Listener and Caregiver are more defined by their intuition and emotions. All four represent a more emotional and supportive team approach to performance, though each highlights a very particular aspect of these attributes.

The top left quadrant, indicated by the caption Emcee, represents the dominant emotional decision-makers whose approach to performance is more directing (self) than team-based. In this quadrant, I introduce the talents of Entertainer, Inspirer, Adapter, and Winner. Employees in this quadrant are upbeat, warm, emotional, and optimistic. They connect well with others, but maintain a clear focus on achieving, primarily as a solo effort. Center stage is a comfortable place for all of the four talents presented in the Emcee quadrant.

Their decisions are made many times by intuition and feelings instead of by empirical thinking; they are comfortable with their emotions and feelings. Roles that are well matched to talents that are exhibited in the Emcee quadrant include sales, retail, performance artists, travel and leisure roles, and support roles that involve a variety of people and are fun.

Employees who test strongly in this quadrant are thoughtful, open, and honest with their feelings and emotions. As direct communicators, they comfortably say what they think. They exhibit upbeat, positive, and encouraging communication; they focus on fun, entertainment, and having a good time. They can be readily identified by their emotional, optimistic, and playful language, and close and engaging body language. They are strong personalities that can easily take charge and direct others. Though they can be successful with others, they are more solo performers who achieve by connecting emotionally with others.

Employees in this quadrant exhibit performance behavior inspired by making more emotional (than strictly rational) decisions and are more interested in solo performance over team performance, though they always show a blend of the two attributes. The talents represented by this quadrant are presented in Figure 2 and are:

- Entertainer – Focuses on fun, feelings, and getting along; upbeat; entertaining and candid; connects with all personalities; spontaneous; conversational, social, and happy; confident and dynamic. Quadrant: Emcee –Feeling/ Directing.

- Inspirer –Brings out the best in others; able to activate, motivate, and inspire others; influential; unites and includes others; visibly present; charismatic and non-judgmental. Quadrant: Emcee – Feeling/Directing.

- <u>Adapter</u> – Is resilient and flexible; easy going and comfortable with change; accommodating and adaptable, accepting; handles many variables at once; focuses on the short term; resilient, responsive, and reactive. Quadrant: Emcee – Directing/Feeling.

- <u>Winner</u> – Needs to win, achieve, and be noticed; pride in great personal achievements; exploits opportunities; inspired by feelings of fame and success; upbeat and optimistic; confident, focused, and engaged. Quadrant: Emcee – Directing/Feeling.

Entertainer and Inspirer are more defined by their feelings and emotions; Adapter and Winner are more defined by their directing (self-oriented) attitude. All four represent an emotional (compared to rational), but more soloist approach to performance, though each highlights a very particular aspect of these attributes.

Below is an alphabetical listing of all sixteen talent topics:

- <u>Adapter</u> – Is resilient and flexible; easy going and comfortable with change; accommodating and adaptable, accepting; handles many variables at once; focuses on the short term; resilient, responsive, and reactive. Quadrant: Emcee – Directing/Feeling.

- <u>Bottom-liner</u> – Focuses on significant performance – exponential instead of incremental; acts with intent; productive and disciplined; thinks carefully and strategically; always results-oriented. Quadrant: Chairman – Thinking/Directing.

- <u>Caregiver</u> – Focuses on emotions and feelings; aware of feelings in self and in others; selfless in service; appreciates and understands individuality; strong sense of belonging, family, and team; openly cares for and supports others;

considerate, empathetic, caring, and compassionate. Quadrant: Friend – Feeling/Supporting.

- Connector – Problem-solving and systemic fact-based focus; connects facts and performance; defines, performs, and lives by goals and objectives; focused and empirical; methodical, logical, and careful. Quadrant: Chairman – Thinking/Directing.

- Driver –Focuses on doing and getting things done; acts with purpose and direction; establishes order; processes many variables concurrently; organizes and delegates; competitive and focused. Quadrant: Chairman – Directing/Thinking.

- Entertainer – Focuses on fun, feelings, and getting along; upbeat; entertaining and candid; connects with all personalities; spontaneous; conversational, social, and happy; confident and dynamic. Quadrant: Emcee –Feeling/ Directing.

- Facilitator – Focuses on learning and teaching others; shares information; advances performance of self and others; detail-oriented; interested in opinions, discussions, and new information; practical thinker. Quadrant: Professor – Supporting/Thinking.

- Includer – Focuses on belonging, contributing, and being part of something important; looks to be understood and appreciated for work and effort; feels connected and helps others feel connected; makes a difference; shares and creates personal contacts; approachable, receptive, sensitive, and loyal. Quadrant: Professor – Supporting/Thinking.

- Inspirer –Brings out the best in others; able to activate, motivate, and inspire others; influential; unites and includes others; visibly present; charismatic and non-judgmental. Quadrant: Emcee – Feeling/Directing.

- <u>Inventor</u> – Independent, creative, and an on-demand thinker; comfortable inventing, imagining, and innovating; considers the non-conventional; easily sees potential, options, and opportunities; interested in new ideas. Quadrant: Professor – Thinking/Supporting.

- <u>Leader</u> – Ability to envision and articulate the future; takes control; able to connect actions to results; strategic thinker; unites, directs, and leads others; intellectual, logical, and focused. Quadrant: Chairman – Directing/Thinking.

- <u>Listener</u> – Communicates clearly and effectively; takes great care to understand and to be understood; understands emotions and feelings; values personal interactions; patient, tolerant, and non-judgmental. Quadrant: Friend – Feeling/Supporting.

- <u>Peacemaker</u> – Gets along with others; avoids confrontation; appreciates feelings, emotions, and differences in people; looks to bring and keep people together; looks for commonalities and agreement; value is in personal contact and relationships; open, kind, and genuine. Quadrant: Friend – Supporting/Feeling.

- <u>Relator</u> – Builds relationships and personal contact; cares about the feelings, lives, and facts of others; enjoys meeting new people and sharing personal experiences; appreciates uniqueness and diversity of people; relaxed, accepting, and supportive. Quadrant: Friend – Supporting/Feeling.

- <u>Solver</u> – Approaches performance and relationships logically; methodical and analytical; addresses performance through fact and information; advances skills to be productive; disciplined approach to work and life; perfectionist mentality. Quadrant: Professor – Thinking/Supporting.

- <u>Winner</u> – Needs to win, achieve, and be noticed; pride in great personal achievements; exploits opportunities; inspired by feelings of fame and success; upbeat and optimistic; confident, focused, and engaged. Quadrant: Emcee – Directing/Feeling.

Now that a language of talents has been presented, it is important to learn how to assess talents and to start using the talent terms in the hiring process to assure that the correct attributes for each role are sourced. When you are clear about the talents required to be successful in each role, you significantly improve the ability to hire an employee who thinks in the way the role requires; this is a critical approach to drive successful intellectual-age performance.

This introduction to talents is presented to create an efficient and reasonable process to define talents; this will then allow your organization to clearly define the thinking and talents need by role. Once defined, you can use the information to source candidates who exhibit the specific talents needed to be successful in each role in the organization. This is the key to Inviting the right employee. The next step is to learn how to assess talents. For that, I introduce the Talent and Thinking Style Assessment™.

## The Talent and Thinking Style Assessment™

It is important to help candidates and employees learn how to define their core talents. This process involves the Talent and Thinking Style Assessment™ that is included with the worksheets printed directly from the website at the beginning of this chapter. This assessment will provide you with a list of attributes. Following the directions, you will assess each line of attributes with a 4 (most like you), to a 1 (least like you). Each line should include a scoring of 4, 3, 2, and 1. Once all rows are scored, add the columns down to calculate a score by column.

These scores will indicate which quadrant(s) most represents the way you think. In some cases, your score will indicate that you are solidly in one quadrant. In other cases, you will find that you exhibit high scores in two quadrants. This may indicate that one of the axes is a more powerful description of you than a quadrant is. Refer to Figure 3. If you score high on both the Chairman and Professor (the vertical line), you are more of a thinker. If you score high on both the Professor and Friend (the horizontal line), you perform best through supporting relationships and engaging others. Similarly, if you score high on both the Friend and Emcee, you perform best through an emotional or intuitive

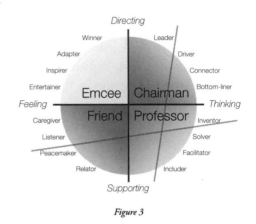

*Figure 3*

approach. If you score high on both the Emcee and Chairman, you are more comfortable directing or solo performing.

Once you locate your highest, or two highest quadrants, assess the talents listed in each. Review the definitions for each of the Fire Up! Talents and determine the four that most represent your natural thinking. To help you define your four primary talents, use the Primary Quadrant and Four Major Talents worksheet you printed from the website at the beginning of this chapter. On this worksheet, notice it asks for your quadrant(s), and then leaves room for you to assess which four of the sixteen talents are most like you. Note that your primary talents are likely to be found in your quadrant(s), but not always. Be sure to review all sixteen talents when assessing your talents. Additionally, to better identify your talents, two more columns are provided. Many times our talents go unnoticed by us; they are simply and naturally the way we think. In this exercise, you must solicit input from two others who know you well. Share your primary quadrant or axis information, and allow two others to define what they feel to be your talents. Record these in the columns indicated by #2 and #3 Assessment. Then, review your summary along with the input of others; circle those talents that you feel to be your four primary talents and record them in the final column on the worksheet.

You have now been introduced to the language of talents. Since talents drive performance in an intellectual workplace, you must be clear about employees' talents and the talents required by each role. The closer these two are matched, the more intellectually connected the employee is to his/her work which will influence his/her engagement level as well.

Time for Practice

From the worksheets you printed for this chapter from the website, access the Talent and Thinking Style Assessment™. Complete this according to the instructions provided on the Assessment. Next, complete Your Quadrant and Four Primary Talents worksheet. This will better introduce you to the language of talents and to your primary four talents. Complete these exercises before moving on.

**Fan the embers – A summary and review**

1. Thinking powers today's economy. Your strongest thinking is referred to as your talents.

2. Talents are unique to each of us; we have a unique combination of talents that are inspired in our early brain development.

3. You can no more control your talents than you can control your gender, race, or other natural

development; they are part of your natural brain development. The goal is then to discover them and maximize them. Success will never happen in trying to add talents that do not exist.

4. Hire for talent; train for skill.

5. Once you discover your talents – your natural learning, yearnings, and interests – you can be better placed in roles that match these to the demands of the role. This encourages an employee's intellectual connection to his/her work.

6. All talents can be summarized by a combination of a thinking or feeling approach to performance, and a directing or supporting approach to performance. Use the Talent and Thinking Style Assessment™ to define your natural thinking and grid quadrant (Chairman, Professor, Friend, or Emcee). Use the quadrants to direct you to the specific talents. Rank those talents that are most like you. Enlist the help of two others who know you well to assist. Define your top four primary talents.

7. Your talents are the same in all aspects of your life – home, work, and leisure. Determining them for the workplace also prepares you to maximize them in life.

*"People don't change that much...Don't try to add in what was left out, try to draw out what was left in."*

Marcus Buckingham
The Gallup Organization

# Chapter 3

## Define What You Need
## The Talent Matrix

**NOTE** Before starting this chapter, go to www.FireUpYourEmployees.com, click on *Beyond the Book*, and print the supporting exercises and worksheets for chapter 3. This text includes the information you need; the website gives you access to the exercises, worksheets, and activities that will help you more fully complete this chapter and advance your learning through practice.

You hire for talents because talents are innate and not trainable (you can develop them, but you can't add them if they don't already exist); it is critical to be clear about the talents needed to succeed in each role. Once the required talents are defined, you will then be able to source and hire the right candidates – those with the right talents. In fact, from this point discontinue the use of the term employee; instead always use the term the right employee. The right employee will always be that employee whose thinking matches the thinking required in his/her role.

Now that you know this and you have a culture that attracts the best candidates, you are ready to put together a definition of what you need by role, to build a sourcing strategy to find the right employees, and to select the best ones in a sound interviewing process; this is how you INVITE the right employee. The process of firing up employees starts with having the right talents (and right employee) in the role. Once that is in place, you can INCITE employees by helping them own their performance through customized roles and performance expectations and IGNITE them to perform by coaching, feedback, and career development.

Before you can INVITE the right employee, you need to be clear about what you are looking for. For that, I introduce the Talent Matrix. This worksheet assembles the required talents (using the list of sixteen presented in chapter 2) along with suggested skills and experience for the role. The Talent Matrix creates a profile of expected performance attributes so an effective robust sourcing strategy to locate candidates who meet these performance and role criteria can be created. To make this an easier process and to assemble all of the needs on one page, review the Talent Matrix included in the exercises and worksheets on the website.

General comment: Talent evaluations are not an exact or empirical assurance of employee fit to a role. Because of the variability in our humanity, there is no precise way to guarantee that an employee will be a great fit for a role. However, a focus on talents introduces the thinking patterns needed to be successful in a role. The more a candidate can exhibit a particular type of thinking, the more information the interviewer has to assess core thinking and first reactions. The presence of the general thinking is only one component of performance; there are many other factors to consider. However, a look at talents and thinking should be the first assessment because in today's intellectual and thinking workplace, how an employee thinks (as evidenced by a talent assessment) will ultimately impact the employee's performance. Though a candidate's talents may not guarantee performance, it will more clearly indicate whether the candidate or employee will be more capable, comfortable, and ultimately happy (based on the work) in a role. Understanding the basic talent types adds greater clarity and information to the hiring process and significantly improves employee placements. The more comfortable you become with talents and the mindsets and behaviors that come with each talent, the more effective you will be in defining the talents that will drive each role in your organization.

Let's return to the Talent Matrix. This Matrix should be completed for each role in the organization so all employees are aware of the talents, skills, and experience that inspire success in each role. The Talent Matrix summarizes the core attributes that can be used to assess current employee fit as well as to create a bias-free profile of the attributes that need to be in place in the interviewing and hiring process. The Talent Matrix assists in bias-free interviewing and hiring because it defines the intellectual or talent requirements without regard to age, gender, ethnicity, religion, or any other protected employee class. No longer is the outside of the employee considered (unless it is through bona fide occupational qualification questions related to lifting, moving, or other physical requirements). This ensures that only candidates that have the right talents (thinking/strengths) are considered; it ensures that the greatest portion of the selection process is objective.

In the Talent Matrix, you first look at talents (role talents and team talents). Though you may like to have all four role talents and two team talents, it is unlikely you will find a candidate with the precise configuration of attributes. Therefore, you will need to define which talents will take priority in your particular workplace. Using a scoring system of one to five (five to indicate most important, and one to indicate least important), evaluate and score the importance of each talent you defined for the role. This will help you decide which talents are most critical for performance and, if not present, that the employee will not be a good fit. This scoring will also be critical to your evaluation process as all candidates will be evaluated as to the degree these talents are present – that number will be multiplied by the importance of the talent to create an overall score for each candidate. I will introduce the Employee/ Candidate Evaluation Matrix in chapter 6.

Once you complete the talents sections, move on to skills. Define the skills (things that have been learned) that will encourage performance. This may include knowledge of certain computer applications, a foreign language, basic accounting or retail math, the fundamentals of customer service, or other performance-related skills. As you did with talents, score the listed skills based on their importance to the role. Skills are important but not as important as talents; skills can be taught if they are missing, while talents cannot be added if they do not naturally exist.

Finally, address experience that may include retail or particular product selling experience, warehouse management, negotiations, leading teams, or other experience. Experience can be important, but history shows that each organization has very particular methods to perform most tasks. In many cases, employees must unlearn some experiences to relearn a new and more organization-focused approach. As you completed for assessing talents and skills, now score the listed experiences based on their importance to the role. This will allow for a more empirical evaluation at the end of the interview process.

In this intellectual economy, how employees think matters most; this is why talents are the first component of Talent Matrix. I spoke of the need for connection – employees must connect *intellectually* to their roles and *emotionally* to their managers. The assessment of the talents, skills, and experience needed in each role helps to create this first level of (intellectual) connection. As you hire employees who are the right fit for the role, you are hiring the way they think. This *thinking*, the ability to handle the requirements of the role, will most significantly influence the success and performance level of the employee.

Let's complete the Talent Matrix together to see it in practice. For this example, let's say you are hiring a retail sales associate. The nature of the job is to handle customers both on the phone and face-to-face, maintain a professional and friendly retail environment, and order product according to customer buying trends. That means you need to analyze both the role and the business to determine the talents that would drive success and performance. This required thinking is most frequently exhibited in the Emcee or Friend quadrants as they have a natural first focus on feelings. Employees who are more emotionally than rationally driven will be more comfortable in roles that greet, deal with, and serve other people. Therefore, we would expect that the core talents that will drive success in this role will come from the Friend and Emcee quadrants.

Because all workplaces are different, the culture of a department or organization will also influence the talents needed to fit into the performance team. So, in addition to the particular role, consider the talents that need to be in place for the employee to fit well on the team or in the workplace. In our example, I'll add that this is a leanly staffed environment that is busy early each day with both foot traffic and phone calls.

As I review the list of sixteen talents, I may identify the following four performance talents (critical to get the job done):

1.  <u>Caregiver</u> – this employee must be good at reading and responding to the needs of people (Quadrant: Friend – Feeling/Supporting).

2.  <u>Relator</u> – this employee must be good at relating to and with others (Quadrant: Friend – Supporting/Feeling).

3.  <u>Listener</u> – this employee must be effective at communicating, understanding, and being understood (Quadrant: Friend – Feeling/Supporting).

4. <u>Inspirer</u> – this employee must be upbeat, positive, and motivate others (Quadrant: Emcee – Feeling/ Directing).

Additionally, because the workplace is fast paced and leanly staffed, all employees must be able to handle many things at once and be able to accommodate change quickly and efficiently, I add two team talents:

1. <u>Bottom-liner</u> – this employee must focus on significant performance, done right the first time (Quadrant: Chairman – Thinking/Directing).

2. <u>Adaptor</u> – this employee must be flexible, comfortable with change, be capable of handing several things at once (Quadrant: Emcee – Directing/Feeling).

List these six talents in the left column on the Talent Matrix. This now becomes a tool to summarize your expectations of the specific talents and natural thinking that will encourage performance in this role. The more closely you match the required thinking with the employee hired, the better chance the employee will not only handle the role well, but fit into the performance culture.

For this role, I then score the importance of each talent. Though I hope to find a candidate with all of these talents, I know that may be improbable. So I focus on the most meaningful of the talents. Based on the review of the role in the particular workplace, I score the talents in the following way:

1. Caregiver – 5

2. Relator – 5

3. Bottom-liner – 4

4. Listener – 4

5. Inspirer – 3

6. Adapter – 2

It is up to you to asses the value of each of the talents based on the factors in your particular workplace. This example tells you that when interviewing (or assessing existing employees), you must first assess for the Caregiver and Relator talents. Any talent that has been assigned a score of five is a must-have talent. If the must-have talent is not assessed to exist in the interview process, then the employee is not a fit and should not be considered. The goal is to make the process more empirical and to improve the ability to hire the right employee now based on clear talent expectations. Being clear about required talents to be successful in the role (those with a score of 5 or 4) also helps to avoid the gut feel and acceptance of candidates that are not a good fit, but are likeable and pleasant. When you hire someone, you are investing in this employee; this employee must demonstrate the thinking that will drive success in his/her role. Again, the focus is on performance and the bottom line.

Once I define the talents needed, I move on to skills. Though skills are less important than talents, they still can add great value. Remember that skills are learned; I can provide training if needed. I should be able to clearly identify the ideal set of skills this employee could have that would help him/her contribute quickly and make an immediate difference.

In my example, I add the following skills and scoring to our Talent Matrix:

1. Speaks Spanish – 5

2. Familiar with product stocking practices and stock rotation – 4

3. Successful with phone skills – 3

4. Able to write effective customer correspondence – 3

5. Able to buy products to meet customer demand – 3

6. Able to use cash registers and manage cash and credit transactions – 2

Again, I would like these if possible, but if a candidate has a great talent fit but does not have these skills, I can provide training. If the skill has a scoring of five and it is not present in the candidate, it is not a requirement to reject the candidate. It means instead that if hired, the new employee will require some immediate education in any of the critical areas (identified with a five).

The third section of the Talent Matrix relates to experience. Experience is, at present, the way most managers assess the fit of the candidate into a role – based on whether he or she has completed some of the functions in the past. Let's stop for a minute and review. You do not pay your employees to just perform the defined functions of their job; rather, you pay them to think about the best, highest service, and most efficient ways of handling workplace situations. If you want a team of employees who are hired to do rote procedures without responsive thinking, then focus your interviewing or employee assessment on previous work experience. But in today's changing workplace, you will never be able to anticipate all of the situations an employee will encounter. Therefore, you must know that when confronted with similar situations (as defined in the role), he/she will think in a dynamic and appropriate way. Experience can add some value, but not in all cases. This is the reason you must focus more on how employees think (talents) – so they can handle situations as they arise instead of just what they have done in the past.

So, with regard to experience on the Talent Matrix, identify the ideal work or life experience that would assist the employee or candidate to be more effective and include scoring. For example:

1. Merchandised product – 5

2. Managed a department – 4

3. Has worked in a retail environment – 3

4. Ordered specialty products – 2

5. Organized a retail showroom or store – 2

As with skills, the lack of a five for one of the experience components is not a reason to specifically reject a candidate. Skills and experiences should become the additional criteria that help to make a clearer choice between several candidates who score at similar levels with regard to talents.

Once the Talent Matrix is completed by role, you have a clearly defined performance profile needed for the role. You now have the ability to:

1. Assess your current workforce and determine how well each employee fits into his/her role.

2. Develop a sound sourcing strategy for any position based on your clearly defined needs to improve the likelihood of finding the right employee.

3. Clearly define the expectations for a new employee to be clear about what you need so the employee will be effective.

This creates the power behind your sourcing strategy: a clear definition and expectation of the talent and other attributes you need to drive performance in the role.

At this point, focus on the process of completing a Talent Matrix for each role in the organization to be clear about what attributes will drive performance. In the talent-based interviewing in chapter 5, you will be introduced to new talent-based interview questions. These power questions look for top-of-mind responses to assess employee talents and will become a more significant part of the interviewing process. In order to create powerful talent-based questions, you will need to be fully aware of the talents and core thinking required in the role. This information will come directly from the completed Talent Matrix.

Things to Consider

- What mechanism does your organization use to assess the performance requirements of each role in the organization?

- Do you currently assess strengths or talents in determining employee fit for roles in the organization?

- What would the response be by employees to determining their talents by use of the Talents and Thinking Style Assessment™?

- How could you help employees see both a personal and professional benefit from learning the language of talents and knowing their most significant talents?

Time for Practice

From the worksheets you printed for this chapter from the website, access the Talent Matrix. This exercise will ask you to complete a Talent Matrix for one role in your organization. Be sure to score the value of each attribute you list on the Talent Matrix. Create your action plan for this chapter including how you will include the Talent Matrix as a key role attribute tool to improve bias-free and performance-based hiring. Complete this exercise before moving on.

## Fan the embers – A summary and review

1. A talent assessment is the most critical component of new employee sourcing or current employee alignment.

2. Use the powerful Talent Matrix to summarize the talents, skills, and experience requirements of each role in the organization.

3. When defining the role's talents, consider both the talents that will drive performance in the role and talents that will encourage a great fit in the team, department, or organization. Remember, hire for talents.

4. When defining skills on the Talent Matrix, identify the ideal skills that would help the employee perform well. Remember, train for skills.

5. Define the ideal experience the role should have; realize that sometimes experience inhibits great performance as a new employee may need to unlearn and relearn products, processes, or other things in order to be effective.

6. Creating a complete Talent Matrix clearly defines the needs of each role. It can then be used to source new talent or to assess the degree of fit of existing talent.

7. The Talent Matrix allows an organization to clearly, and without bias, identify the attributes that are required to be successful in a role. And since talents are intrinsic (not external), the problematic biases that enter into employee hiring and advancement can be avoided.

*"Have a bold and
blatant disregard for
normal constraints."*
Steve Farber

# Chapter 4

## Find the Right Employee
## Develop a Robust
## Sourcing Strategy

**NOTE** Before starting this chapter, go to www.FireUpYourEmployees.com, click on *Beyond the Book*, and print the supporting exercises and worksheets for chapter 4. This text includes the information you need; the website gives you access to the exercises, worksheets, and activities you will need to fully complete this chapter and to advance your learning through practice.

You are in a war for talent – now and for some time to come. With the retiring Baby Boomers, the shift of manufacturing offshore, changes in Homeland Security policies affecting the supply of immigrant workers, the slowdown in skill training, the shift to intellectual or service work, and fewer and fewer employees feeling connected or engaged in their work, you have an impending employment challenge. Some call this the perfect storm – a significant quality-employee supply event ready to significantly affect every workplace unless we take know-how to prepare for and weather this challenge.

This congruence of issues affects all organizations in the following ways:

- There are less developed skills in the existing employees.
- There is, and will be, greater competition for each employee.

- Workplaces will have to learn to be more flexible and nimble to respond to changes more quickly.

- Getting an employee will be important – keeping the employee will be critical.

- All employees will need to be involved in the search and recruiting process.

- Recruiting and sourcing talent must be a daily event.

The last two bullets are the starting point for this chapter. With the current mix of issues affecting our workplace, you have to change your perspective about locating and sourcing talent. Strictly placing an ad, reviewing several resumes, and hiring based on convenience will not consistently source the best candidate. It is a completely new and different workplace. Chapter 5 will introduce a more robust interview process and the concept of talent-based questions, but until then, you need to develop a process to constantly locate and source the right employees.

Key to hiring the right employee is a requirement that organizations develop a robust sourcing strategy; this is a strategic process that constantly anticipates position and skill needs and builds in a response to find candidates who will match these needs. Now you can see the value of a powerful employee-focused culture that was presented in chapter 1. This kind of culture attracts the attention of high potential candidates; it becomes the workplace brand that employees want to be part of. It earns the organization the status employer of choice.

As I presented, you need to have many candidates to be able to make the right choice. The right employee is an employee whose talents match the talents required in the role and may have some of the skills and experience preferred. Without a good choice of candidates, there is a great chance you will be forced to select from the few candidates that show up, all of whom may not be right for the role. Using what you know about the need to intellectually and emotionally connect each employee to his/her role to activate extraordinary performance, you cannot just place any person in any role and achieve the level of performance needed. To find the right employee, you must attract the best and ultimately select the best. For that, we need choice.

## Things to Consider

- What draws employment candidates to your organization?

- What is your organization's current sourcing strategy?

- How effective is it in locating legitimate and highly qualified (right) employment candidates?

## Find the Good Ones

From the Talent Matrix, you have created the attributes you need for each role in the organization. This is a great starting point to create a robust sourcing strategy that continually locates the best candidates and maintains a pipeline of contacts and candidates to respond to future needs and opportunities. Remember, sourcing great candidates should not be limited to those times when a vacancy exists. In today's intensely competitive and intellectual workplace, sourcing future talent must be a daily event. All employees must know what talents the organization is looking for, make constant contacts with viable employment candidates, and be involved in searching for quality future employees. All employees must now own the process of helping to create a powerful team of employees, well cast into the right roles. The more management engages and activates employees to be part of this process, the more successful the organization can be in locating great potential candidates and ensuring that contacts exist when needs arise.

The process of hiring for talents naturally forces all organizations to advance their diversity initiatives to assess candidates based on thinking and contribution; it forces organizations to consider all employees, regardless of previous history or cultural behaviors. Today's employees' talents may show up in any variety of employee backgrounds; organizations that have significant diversity initiatives consider a wider population of applicants from which to assess talents. This allows these organizations to continue to hire on talent because they consider sources and candidates that do not look or act like those who are currently employed. This diversity provides greater employee choice, improved chances of finding the right combination of talents, and more varied experiences and perspectives that now become included in the mindset of the organization. This movement to an intellectual workplace has positively affected all employees as it has eliminated many of the glass ceilings imposed on the protected classes of age, gender, religion, ethnicity, race, disability, or any other bias. Today's intellectual workplace is a defense of diversity.

Robust employee sourcing now requires that all organizations build a talent pool that transcends job requisitions; sourcing is now a recurring critical component of running a business and is a daily event. Consider the following fundamentals when creating a robust sourcing strategy:

1. Always know what you need and what you are looking for (talents, skills, experience – source your talent from the details of the Talent Matrix).

2. Always know where candidates who possess the specific talents you need work, study, shop, or live.

3. Live a daily sourcing contact plan; ensure that sourcing is a daily or weekly discussion. Build into everyone's jobs a component of recruiting, educating, and investing for the future; all employees should become recruiters for the organization.

4. Share employment news, needs, and opportunities with employees so they know how to be a part of the recruiting effort.

5. Reward those who participated in finding successful candidates.

6. Meet regularly to brainstorm unconventional ideas to find key talents; use all forms of technology as well as word-of-mouth to locate potential candidates. Partner with schools, host in-house programs to introduce the organization to the area.

7. Regularly reinvent the sourcing process to ensure it stays innovative, responsive, and effective. Build a robust candidate section of the organization's website that is clever, entertaining, powerful, and attractive. Make it easy for new employees to apply and for existing employees to move within the organization.

8. Develop your diversity population through neighborhood associations, immigrant liaisons, churches, and other groups who matriculate immigrant workers. Focus on the talents required and learn to welcome and appreciate the significant benefits that come with employees with diverse backgrounds and rich heritages.

Sourcing strategies must be flexible to accommodate the specifics of the industry and the events of the day. Significant employee involvement, creative approaches, and intense information sharing are the critical components of an organization's successful sourcing strategy. Today, everything must be considered. Standard approaches bring standard results. Success requires clever, creative, and responsive approaches that locate and attract those who are best qualified for each role.

Things to Consider

1. What do your employees think about participating in locating talent for the organization?

2. What is your organization's current external recruiting strategy? How successful is it?

3. What is the role of each team member in your recruiting or sourcing strategy? Why?

4. What is the most unconventional thing your organization has considered to source new talent? Did the organization implement it? If so, was it effective?

5. How will the shift to sourcing talent (not just experience and skills) change your approach to finding the right employee for the right role?

Sourcing new talent is always a challenge. The Fire Up! Process[SM] introduces the Role Sourcing Strategy worksheet to direct a more defined and effective approach. Refer to the copy to the Role Sourcing Strategy worksheet included in the worksheets for chapter 4 found on the website www.FireUpYourEmployees.com.

**Role Sourcing Strategy Worksheet Completion Instructions:**

Page one:

- Start first with the three top performance talents (per your ranking on the Talent Matrix) for a specific role. For each of these talents, identify where people with these talents live, work, shop, or congregate. How do people with these talents communicate, contact each other, what do they watch, and if they are looking for work, what sources would they review? Where might you see these people performing at their best? Develop your locations to source this talent for each of the three performance (to complete the job) talents.

- Move on to one of the top team talents (a talent that will encourage a good fit on your team) per your ranking on the Talent Matrix. Use the same thinking as above to identify the locations to source this talent.

Page two:

- Move on to skills and experience. Review the critical components of each and identify where you would find people who have these skills and experience. Consider and list any location to find these skills and experience.

- Based on page one and the top of page two, start to create a specific sourcing plan for this role.
    —Identify the conventional methods to attract and locate candidates who are a good fit.
    —Identify unusual or unconventional methods to attract and locate candidates who are a good fit.

- Define the roles of employees in the sourcing process. This could include brainstorming, researching, contacting, or participating. Encourage a broad support of sourcing.

Consider creating this sourcing strategy for all key roles in the organization. Remember, the time to source talent is not just when there is an opening or immediate need. Talent sourcing must be a regular event and it is more effective and widely accepted if it works from a plan that defines its approach, location, and responsibilities. This way, employees know their role in the process, the approach can be evaluated for effectiveness, and a pipeline of the right employees can be developed to respond to immediate or future needs.

Time for Practice

From the worksheets you printed for this chapter from the website, locate the Role Sourcing Strategy worksheet. This exercise will ask you to complete a Role Sourcing Strategy worksheet for one actual role in your organization. Using the Talent Matrix that you prepared in chapter 3, now complete a corresponding Role Sourcing Strategy worksheet. Work with your team to access their perspectives about sourcing. Allow them to brainstorm – particularly about the non-conventional locations to source this particular role (not only will this add more options to consider, but to be included in this process is very empowering for employees). Create your action plan for this chapter including how you will include the Role Sourcing Strategy worksheet as a tool to locate the right talent and create a pipeline of talent for the future.

**Fan the embers – A summary and review**

1. Today's workplace requires a more clever and innovative sourcing strategy; bland, generic recruiting is ineffective. Recruiting must be specific and be based on the profile established on the Talent Matrix.

2. All employees must become recruiters for the organization. Employees are the eyes and ears of all organization; sharing your Talent Matrix hiring needs will prepare employees to notice talents in others and start the process of driving attention to the organization.

3. All forms of technology, as well as word-of-mouth, are to be considered to locate potential candidates. Know all of the sources for on-line resumes or job postings and maintain creatively-worded ads. Consider social networks, share key information, define yourself as a "talent" organization (insist that all applicants submit "talent-based" resumes).

4.  Traditional and non-traditional forms of advertising should be used to attract candidates from all sources.

5.  Partner with schools. Offer to teach at local trade schools, colleges, and universities. Set up internships, endowments, and other connections between the organization and the educational institution to be able to access the best and brightest students. Offer to mentor students and younger employees.

6.  Build a powerful and easy to access Internet hiring and career opportunity site on your organization's website. Develop an interesting, robust, and value-add site that attracts a great amount of interest in your organization and your positions.

7.  Develop your diversity population. Start to consider locations to find and attract immigrants, the disabled, women, military, and others who are not always initially considered.

8.  Use the Role Sourcing Strategy worksheet to organize, customize, and brainstorm an effective talent locating process for each specific role. The structure of the worksheet encourages employees to know their roles in the process, evaluate the approach for effectiveness and clearly develop a pipeline of the right employees to respond to immediate or future needs.

"*Choose a job you love,
and you'll never work
a day in your life.*"
*Confucius*

# Chapter 5

## Hire the Best
## A Progressive
## Interview Process

**NOTE** Before starting this chapter, go to www.FireUpYourEmployees.com, click on *Beyond the Book*, and print the supporting exercises and worksheets for chapter 5. This text includes the information you need; the website gives you access to the exercises, worksheets, and activities you will need to fully complete this chapter and to advance your learning through practice.

You have clearly defined what talents you need in each role in the organization. You have created a powerful role sourcing strategy that locates the right candidates. You have created an employee-focused culture that attracts and INVITES the best to apply. The result of this is that you now have choice. Choice will be critical in the process of hiring the right employee.

Next comes a comprehensive eight-step hiring process designed to ensure that all steps to effective hiring are completed in the most meaningful order. Though, in practice, several of these steps may be combined, be aware of the need for each step as it helps to assure that when you hire, you hire the right employee.

Before we proceed, let's again review who the right employee is and why it is so critical to hire only the right employee. This employee has the talents that match the talents and thinking required in the particular role. Though skills and experience are valuable, the focus must first be on making a thinking and talent match. This works to establish a strong intellectual connection between the employee and the job. Studies show that this connection, coupled with the emotional connection to the manager, is what engages employees to perform at their best.

In today's intellectual workplace, the right employee is one who is well suited to the role. This improves the likelihood that the employee will be interested in what he/she does and, therefore, perform better. In a service workplace, employees are the face of the organization to customers – the more engaged, connected, and happy employees are in their work, the more they connect with customers. Connecting with customers builds relationships, impacts loyalty, and ultimately drives results. Selecting an employee who is capable of this is critical to the success of the organization. It starts with a comprehensive hiring process that clearly defines the talents, skills, and experience the role requires, accesses a powerful pipeline of candidates, and interviews in a new and more results-oriented way to fully understand each candidate's thinking before you make the hiring decision.

In the industrial age, many employee roles were interchangeable. In an intellectual workplace, there is a greater need for each employee to be the right fit for the role since not all employees think alike. Today's hiring practice must be capable of assessing talents so the organization can invest wisely in its intellectual capital (its employees).

This comprehensive hiring process includes the following steps; each will be developed more completely in the following pages:

> **Step 1:** Establish and define the need – Clearly define the employment or task needs and whether hiring or role realignment is required.

**Step 2:** Create the Talent Matrix – Create or update the Talent Matrix for each role that clearly defines the required talents and the expected skills and experience.

**Step 3:** Use the Talent Matrix: Conduct an internal search, then external search – Successful organizations first look within the organization to encourage growth. Remember that the Talent Matrix is still the standard for hiring; if existing employees do not have the required talents to be successful, then the search moves externally. Once you complete the internal search, conduct an external search to round out the number of candidates or if the internal search did not yield the right candidates.

**Step 4:** Review resumes and job applications – Review to determine first round talent fit. Cover the names to focus on talents not on gender, ethnicity, or any other bias. In today's workforce, the additional benefit of hiring for talent is that it generally brings in a more diverse team of employees. The more diverse, the greater their experiences and the more perspectives they offer to the organization. Select those that fit your need for phone and/or face-to-face follow up.

**Step 5:** Conduct a pre-qualifying, pre-visit telephone interview – Contact the potential candidates to assess the first impressions about talent and fit and to rule out applicants who cannot meet the bona fide occupational qualifications.

**Step 6:** Host a face-to-face interview – Host a face-to-face "investing" interview that has a plan to gather specific information about the candidates' talents, skills, and experience that met bona fide occupational qualifications and responded well in the pre-interview phone call.

**Step 7:** Evaluate the interview candidates – Conduct a review and evaluation process that has input from all of those in the interviewing process. Use the Candidate/Employee Evaluation Matrix to impartially assess each candidate and to create a bias-free, intellectual hiring approach.

**Step 8:** Candidate selection and final offer – Make a formal selection from all qualified applicants and present a formal written offer of employment.

This chapter will review steps one through five, including presenting a new approach to talent-based interviewing and using talent-based questioning. Chapter 6 will present steps six through eight. Chapter 7 will present a first day and week on-boarding process to hook the new employee into performance from the outset.

**Step 1 - Establish and Define the Need**

The first step in my process to hire the right employee determines whether a need for hiring truly exists; this decision requires information. Develop a process to assess the responsibilities that belonged to a departing employee or the responsibilities that exist for a new role. If looking to replace an employee, it is now time to review the previous job description and Talent Matrix on the role. If this position continues to add value and/or drive results, the position will likely need to remain. Many times the departure of an employee allows for a minor (or major) restructuring of responsibilities that both activates existing employees to greater roles and better aligns responsibilities to other employees. In this event, the review may indicate that there is no need for hiring.

Review the following questions and use them to determine if what is needed is a realignment of duties or a new employee.

- What has prompted the need to consider a change or new employee?

- Can the tasks be completed by another employee who is right for the role?

- What will be the responsibilities of this new position – what talents are needed?

- Are these talents available in the current workforce?

- How will this position affect the profitability of the location, department, or organization?

- How does the position fit into the organization or department's mission?

- Could this position be restructured to be done on a part-time basis?

- What are the primary and secondary responsibilities of this position?

- What are the required technical skills?

- What emotional impact will this role have on customers?

- To whom will this position report?

- Have performance standards, performance expectations, or a job description been created for this role?

- What is the timing for a change with this position?

- What is the lead time for either an internal or external search?

- If a new employee is needed, what is the status of the hiring process for this position?

This process should include observation, review, questioning, and analysis to be able to prove a true employment need. Once the decision to hire has been made, this analysis will clearly define talents, skills, experience, and attitude needed to be successful in the position

If a new position has been created, it is still important to complete the previous review to determine whether the new position is required or if it can be successfully absorbed by existing staff. This process is required to determine if hiring is the right response. If not, realign positions, meet with employees, and monitor changes. If hiring is the right response, move on to Step 2 – Create the Talent Matrix.

Time for Practice

From the worksheets you printed for this chapter from the website, access the worksheet marked Step 1. Complete your work on this worksheet. This exercise will ask you to review your latest position vacancy (employee was fired or gave notice) and define your assessment process to rehire or realign the role. Consider the questions provided and determine if your outcome would have changed. Add any action items to your Action Plan as they relate to assessing rehiring or realignment for vacant roles. Complete this activity before moving on.

## Step 2 - Create the Talent Matrix

You can easily create the specific job requirements, job description, and performance standards for any job in the organization. This still doesn't ensure that you will hire the right employee. Simply being capable of the job requirements misses a significant part of the hiring process. As I presented earlier, we train for skills, but hire for talent. That means you must identify the talents that are required to do the job well. Does this position need to be comfortable dealing with all types of people or does the position require a great analytical mind? Does the position require a take charge individual or someone who works quietly behind the scenes?

Let's review what should be considered when creating the Talent Matrix:

- Create the job description and overall responsibilities.
  —Why? To clearly define what is expected and to be fair and consistent with all applicants.

- Identify the required talents (thinking).
  —Why? To define the thinking required to ensure success in the role. As I stated, consider identifying four talents directed to the thinking for the role and two talents that will ensure a better fit into the organization or team. Notice that I say talents, not personalities. When you clearly define the talents, you fully understand the role and how the role must think to be successful; this allows you the ability to source (invest in) the right person for the role.

- Identify the ideal skills for the role.
  —Why? To indicate the skills that will help the hired candidate feel immediately capable and competent in the role. Additionally, it defines the skill set so it can be applied fairly and evenly through all hiring decisions. Though important, it is not as important as the talents section since skills can be taught; employees can learn new skills as compared with talents that are core and part of our natural thinking. Also consider bona fide occupational qualifications (BFOQ). Bona fide occupational qualifications refer to the specific

qualifications that are a required component of a particular role. The way to develop the BFOQ or job qualifications is to review the job description and create the required core or fundamental skills needed to successfully perform the role. Generally, BFOQ will relate to the specific functions of a role, such as lifting or driving requirements, certifications, or performance levels. These may not affect talent areas, but any BFOQ requirement must be considered in reviewing a candidate before talents, other skills, and experience are considered. If a role requires the employee to be able to lift a certain number of pounds and the candidate cannot lift the weight, the candidate must not be considered regardless of his/her talent fit. Start with the mandated role requirements to rule candidates in or out. If they can meet the role's bona fide occupational qualifications, and they have the talents required for the role as defined on the Talent Matrix, they can be considered for interviewing. BFOQ must be consistently applied to all applicants without bias.

Clear BFOQ qualifications do the following:

- They define specific skills that may be required in a particular role.

- They encourage uniformity in hiring standards to eliminate subjective and possibly discriminatory practices by employers.

- They create a mechanism to allow or disallow candidates based on a first level of job fit, applied without bias.

By clearly defining the skills required to be successful in the role, which includes any BFOQ qualifications, you are preparing yourself for effective, fair, and discrimination-free hiring, and an employee who has the ability to be successful in his/her role.

- Identify the ideal experience and background for the role.
  —Why? To define the work experience that will add additional value for the candidate and shorten the learning curve to be successful in the role. Additionally, it defines the skill set so it can be applied fairly and evenly through all hiring decisions. Though important, it is not as important as the talents section since in many cases, experience is unique to a particular organization and the new employee frequently must unlearn behaviors to be successful in a new environment.

Prepare a Talent Matrix

The best way to create the profile of what is needed in the role is to complete the Talent Matrix introduced in chapter 3. The completed Talent Matrix clearly defines the talents, skills, and experience that will drive success in the role and helps to source an employee who will be a good fit.

## Step 3 – Use the Talent Matrix: Conduct an internal search, then external search.

Now that you are clear about what attributes you need in this new or existing role, you can start to locate candidates. First, start with an internal review. If the right employee does not exist internally, you will need to start an external search.

Though you have learned how to develop a robust (external) sourcing strategy in chapter 4, always initiate your search internally. Progression from within is extremely effective in building employee morale, commitment, and loyalty. All searches for new positions or changed positions should start with a review of current staffing; an internal search is also part of a robust sourcing strategy. First, considering your people sends an important message about your workplace culture; it shows that you value them, care about them, and invest in them. Employees are assets, not expenses. Considering an internal candidate first (subjected to the same review for matching talent to role) not only ensures the employee's potential for success in the role and shows you actively promote from within to advance talented employees, but to be successful, the selection consideration must still follow the process of hiring for talent.

Consider the following sources when starting an internal search.

- Manager trainee program employees – graduates and those currently in the program.

- Future manager list from a succession planning or development initiative (more on this in chapter 10).

- Other sources – contact human resources or other managers throughout the organization.

- Internal postings through newsletters, the organization's career website, or other methods.

- Networking at organization's events including training programs, meetings, and public events.

When ready to post for a role, consider the following:

- Clearly identify the position and performance expectations.

- Clearly identify the talents required to be successful.

- Clearly identify the skills and experience preferred.

- Create a clear response process so those who are interested can easily submit required information. Remember, the easier the application process, the more likely it is that employees will apply. If the application process is complex, time consuming, or difficult, employees will not take the time. An easy application process will then influence your workplace brand and impact your reputation in the market.

Remember that a strong employee-focused organization committed to its employees regards its employees well enough to actively promote them to environments that match their thinking and talents. It is imperative that all internal responses for job postings be reviewed seriously and timely. Word gets around quickly if the organization does not openly encourage promotion and employee movement. Many managers work hard to hold on to their high performing employees, making the process of movement or advancement difficult. Powerful employee-focused cultures value constant growth and challenge for all employees and, thereby, make it easy to respond to opportunities within the organization. But, it must be formally stated that only employees who are the right fit for an opportunity will be considered. Having a completed Talent Matrix helps to show all employees the requirements of the role and they can then determine their fit. This creates a more powerful and openly fair workplace. It also maintains a stated standard that only the right employees will be considered for the roles.

## Things to Consider

- What works well in your organization's current internal sourcing strategy? What doesn't work well? Why?

- How do your employees currently feel about applying for positions from within? Is the process easy or difficult from the employee's perspective?

- Do employees know of all opportunities as they become available? Does management provide the Talent Matrix list of expectations, talents, skills, and experience they are looking for in the role?

## Move to External

Sometimes the right employee will not be in your current workforce; your sourcing must then be directed outside of the organization. In many applications, an outside employee is of great value because he/she:

- Is not familiar with culture and procedures, so new ideas may be considered.

- Is not familiar with the industry to follow history instead of inventing new approaches and considering new possibilities.

- Has a history in another industry and can bring new and meaningful perspectives to your organization.

- Successfully challenges all decisions to see that they are meaningful and purposeful instead of doing what has always been done.

As we saw in chapter 4, successful organizations are always sourcing talent; they are always gathering names, talking to businesses, hosting seminars, partnering with schools, hosting job fairs, and using many other ways to promote their employment brand and employee-focused culture. This assures direct contact with areas and organizations that can source employee leads as well as create a list of potential candidate names to check with as vacancies become available.

The process of sourcing great talent belongs to all employees. Imagine the connective power of all employees engaged in finding future employees because they know the talents, skills, and experience the organization needs. They now become recruiters for the organization. They become workplace brand ambassadors. With so many more focused on the process of constantly identifying viable candidates, the candidate pipeline quickly fills. This provides the critical choice that organizations need to find the right employee.

Done well, at this point there will be both internal and external candidate names to consider. Some of the names may have been solicited, others may have seen a very specific ad or opportunity posting. Either way, you now have quality candidates to review. The next step is to get more details on each to determine which should advance in the process and which should be directed to other opportunities.

Time for Practice

From the worksheets you printed for this chapter from the website, access the worksheet marked Step 3. Complete your work on this worksheet. This exercise asks you to assess and develop an internal review process to source the position for which you completed a Talent Matrix in chapter 3. How would you locate internal talent for this role? We have already reviewed creating an external sourcing strategy in chapter 4. Complete this activity before moving on.

## Step 4 – Review Resumes and Job Applications

Let's stop and review this process to date. You have assessed whether there was a need to hire, and if so, you have created a Talent Matrix to define the specific talents, skills, and experience needed. You have first checked within your organization as to whether you have a match for your need. Even if you find a great internal candidate, you may still search externally because you are always interested in the best candidate. True, you give your internal employees the first consideration, but your focus is still hiring the right employee for the right role. When you have more choice, you encourage a better hire.

You have now sourced job applications or resumes for your open position. And when done well, you now have hard copies and electronic information about the attributes of employment candidates. Next, develop a process of reviewing this information to locate the right candidates to contact via phone for a pre-interview call and ultimately, for those who seem the best fit, a face-to-face interview.

There are many ways to review the information that applicants send. Remember that in today's intellectual workplace, you are truly more interested in the applicants' talents, then skills, then experience. You have no particular interest in the applicant's gender, age, race, ethnicity, or color, unless it is affects a particular bona fide occupational qualification for the role. At this point, you need a reliable process to assess how candidates think. That means you must be able to assess the information you receive as an indicator of the candidates' talents.

As of today, most resumes are experience-based. Candidates add general details about roles they have had or things they have done. Very little of this helps the interviewer or resume/application reviewer really understand how the candidate thinks. Candidates' previous work experience may not necessarily tell much about thinking or talents; the candidate may have hated the role he/she was in, performed poorly, or made no difference. That means that many of the attributes listed on today's resumes offer no significant or meaningful guidance about candidate thinking and whether this thinking is appropriate for the open role.

I have introduced, to all the organizations I work with, a new talent-based resume format (you can see this new resume format for the resume created for my fictitious employee "Hans Furhigher," included in the resource pages for chapter 5, downloaded from the website www.FireUpYourEmployees. com). This new format moves away from the experience- and skill-based resumes that make it more difficult for interviewers to assess the candidate's intrinsic thinking and talents. In an intellectual economy, employees are paid for what and how they think; a review of talents is critical in intellectual-age interviews to assess and prove candidates' talents. A talent-based resume makes this process more successful.

When reviewing the more pervasive skill- and experience-based resumes, start first by an assessment of responsibilities and information provided; determine if this information provides any insight into employee thinking. If so, and the talents or thinking they exhibit match the talents needed, they make the first cut – move these applications or resumes to the left; all others move to the right. Those in the right-hand stack must be contacted to inform them they do not match the thinking required in the role and will be considered for other roles that are more in line with their talents. This creates a professional and positive response in the mind of the applicant. Though not a good fit for the current role, they should be maintained as an interested party to be considered for other or future roles. This should be part of the organization's sourcing strategy.

Using the applications/resumes that were moved to the left, assess their skills and experience against the skills and experience on the role's Talent Matrix. Again, move those that match in more of the higher priority skills and experience to the left, discarding those that do not match well to the right. This should leave you with the resumes or applications that should be subjected to a brief phone interview. The purpose of the interview will be to get a preliminary sense of talents (thinking) and to verify that any BFOQ or required performance can be done such as lifting, speaking, driving, or any other aspect of the job that requires a particular skill or certification. You can see that this process holds all applicants to a particular standard without bias. All applicants are subjected to the same Talent Matrix criteria.

The purpose of this step is to reduce the population of responses to a meaningful group worthy of follow-up. Now that we understand the process, let's spend a little time on what to look for on the resume or application. This process becomes significantly easier the more applicants move from skill-based to talent-based resumes. Then the process will be more a match to the Talent Matrix, and the time spent in the interview will be to verify the presented talents exist. Until then, let's take a look at resumes and how to start to review them for the presence of talents. It will be important to look through the verbiage on the resume or application to assess the experience and skills as indicators of talents. In many cases this will be our only introduction to the candidate's thinking until we contact him/her via phone.

The resume

A traditional resume is a summary of work and professional experience (not talents) that is presented to give a brief summary of the capabilities and accomplishments of a candidate. The resume contains educational information, specific work and task experience, and professional performance in activities, organizations, or other events. Treat the resume as an introduction to the candidate and to determine which candidates will be invited to a phone or face-to-face interview. Again, you are more interested in their talents, which may be difficult to assess with a traditional resume.

It is fair for you to request that applicants submit talent-based resumes. Consider posting a sample talent-based resume on your website. Again, review the resume that was created for my fictitious employee "Hans Furhigher" as an example of a talent-based resume (included in your resources for chapter 5 downloaded from the website www.FireUpYourEmployees. com). The more candidates prepare a resume that supports how they think, the easier the process of assessing their fit in your organization and role will be. In the absence of a talent-based resume, review the positions held for the talents they exhibit. List the talents you perceive from their positions and experience. This may be enough to bring them in for a face-to-face interview with true talent-based questions that will assess the talents you are looking for.

Besides a look for talents, use the resume to assess the following:

- <u>Sense of strengths</u> – Assess activities, interests, awards, and accomplishments as sources of additional strengths that may not be used in current work but are resident in the candidate.

- <u>Work history</u> – Review the progression showing performance improvement, type of work, and gaps in work. What does this tell you about the employee? What questions does it bring to mind that will need answering if the employee is interviewed?

- <u>Work experience</u> – Review the variety in tasks, specializations, interests, and accomplishment as an indication of capabilities.

- <u>Sense of direction</u> – Assess overall work direction and its indication of career direction.

Review the resume to get a preliminary feeling about the applicant. And, as you can imagine, you need to rely on the presented information. Approximately 45 percent of candidates state their resumes are not entirely accurate, which is why it is so important to verify as much of the critical information as possible. The latest statistics support the cost of a bad hire to be approximately 25 – 200 percent of the employee's salary. This is a reminder that you must invest in your employees by taking the time to define what you need, interview wisely, and prove the candidates have what you need. If the wrong employee is hired, the impact on the organization, team, morale, customer relationships, and bottom line can be significant.

Since resumes contain a significant amount of information, use the worksheet included in your resources for chapter 5 downloaded from the website www.FireUpYourEmployees.com with the following four caption headings – Comments, Missing Information, Meaningful Experience (and Skills), and Sense of Talents – to review and assess information presented on resumes.

## 1. Comments

List the comments or questions you have when reviewing the resume or application. These will be things to comment on if the candidate is selected for an interview or questions that will need follow-up because of something you read or expected to read on the resume/application. In your review process:

- Watch for generalities.

- Watch for logic in job progression and job continuity – what does it tell you about the way the applicant thinks? What areas are applicants naturally drawn to? Away from?

- Watch for unreasonable gaps in employment as potential indicators of the candidate's ability to stay committed to a role or team.

- Watch for unreasonable accomplishments or skills – what does this tell you about how the applicant works, how he/she fits in, and the applicant's opinion of self?

- Watch for inaccuracies, errors, and outright false statements – you are investing in someone who will represent you to the customer regardless of the role. Remember your organization's mission and ethical code. All of these must be considered to determine if the applicant will be a fit.

- Watch for vague words such as
    —Assisted in.
    —Helped with.
    —Coordinated.
    —Involved with.

    These words hide the real level of participation. Again, the goal is to know fact – to know exactly the way the employee thinks and the things that he/she has done. Vague words disguise true accomplishments and the only way to INVITE the right person is to know what the candidate has actually done.

- Define the first cutoff criteria (based on job description, BFOQ, and talent assessment). Watch for things that take applicants out of the running. For instance, if the role required a particular class of driving license and the skills section of the resume did not have the required license listed, the resume must be disregarded.

## 2. Missing information
List the gaps or inconsistencies that need follow-up. List any information you expected to see but did not. This will help to direct your questions should you decide to advance this candidate to the interview process.

## 3. Meaningful experience (and skills)
Of the work experience or skills presented, identify those that are meaningful to you based on your Talent Matrix. This will

define the areas you will want to corroborate if the candidate is selected for an interview; if you want to rely on information presented on a resume or application, you must verify it through questioning in the interview or through outside confirmation.

### 4. Sense of talents

If the resume is an experience-based resume, identify the sense of talents that the work experience indicates (this process is easier if a talent-based resume is submitted). Defining this will help to compare it against the talents you identified on your Talent Matrix. If the talents seem close, and the other criteria are met, it may help to identify the candidate as a potential for an interview. You can then assess your sense of talents by using the talent-based questions that are presented in chapter 6.

Here are some of the don'ts (so that all applicants are treated fairly, consistently, and legally):

- Never write on the resume. Make your comments on the Talent Matrix or Employee/Candidate Evaluation Matrix (presented in chapter 6). Remember that all notes can be subpoenaed if any suit or legal action about the hiring is brought.

- Never make written personal comments about protected classes, personalities, or appearances on your notes. The interview must be fair and impartial – comments about gender, religion, age, and race are not only illegal, but they distract the process of assessing candidates on talents and will create significant consequences for an organization if hiring decisions are challenged legally. This Process is designed to create a consistently bias-free approach to hiring the right employee. Bias and discriminatory comments have no place in an interview that is looking to invest in the right employee for the organization.

- Disregard the candidate's name as you start your resume review. Natural bias for or against a particular gender or nationality may create a sense of discrimination. Review the content of the resume without regard to the candidate's identity and review each resume the same way.

The resume or application is the first introduction to the candidate. Be fully aware of what you need in the role (Talent Matrix) as you start your review. Apply the same criteria to all resumes, looking for fit and whether the candidate is worth your investment. To ensure this, you must know which attributes will help the candidate be successful in the role and then have a process to assess whether these attributes exist (strongly enough or at all) to INVITE the employee for an interview.

## Things to Consider

- What is the greatest risk in your organization's resume or job application review process? Why?

- How do you/will you successfully handle this risk and select the right candidates to interview?

- What do you think of the idea of a talent-based resume?

- How will you encourage candidates to submit only talent-based resumes for opportunities with your organization?

## Time for Practice

From the worksheets you printed for this chapter from the website, access the worksheet marked Step 4 and the two sample resumes. Complete your work on the worksheet marked Step 4. This exercise will ask you to review two resumes – one is presented in the usual experience-based format (the candidate is Mia DiWun), the other introduces a new talent-based format (the candidate is Hans Furhigher). Review the resumes with the approach presented in this chapter (comments, missing information, meaningful experience, and sense of talents). Start your process of a more focused review of resumes to improve your employee selection process. Complete this activity before moving on.

### Step 5 – Conduct a Pre-qualifying, Pre-visit Telephone Interview.

The goal of the application/resume review process is to fairly and legally identify who should proceed to the next level in the hiring process – the phone interview. This is also the time you should start to consider the phone interview questions; the same questions must be asked to all phone interview applicants. If the questions are not the same, it can be construed as bias. Therefore, your questions should be talent-based, BFOQ-based, and appropriate for all of your applicants who have made it to this stage of the hiring process.

Statistics show the following:

- The goal for pre-visit telephone interviews is ten candidates. It will probably require a review of thirty or more resumes to find ten worth submitting to the next step of the process. Though this is a guide, your actual situation will determine how many to review. At this stage, think in terms of the ratio 3:1 – resumes reviewed to scheduled phone interviews.

- Phone interviewing ten applicants should create four to five face-to-face interview candidates.

- Four to five face-to-face candidates will yield two top talent choices.

- These figures are approximates and a guide; your industry and the nature of the position may vary. What matters most is having a choice, and to have the choice needed to locate the right employee, you must create an attracting workplace culture and clear set of performance requirements (talents). The more attracting your culture is, the more likely you will be able to attract enough candidates to allow yourself the choice you need to find and the employee who is right for the role.

## Key pre-visit telephone interview questions

First, consider the bona fide occupational qualification (BFOQ) questions – these are questions that will immediately include or exclude a candidate from consideration. If you reviewed the resumes and have found ten that you feel capable of meeting the profile identified on the Talent Matrix, check to see if any must be ruled out for a particular performance (skill) reason – this includes lifting, language, driving, etc. Though you may have included the bona fide occupational qualifications on the job description, it is still wise to start your phone interview by ensuring that the candidates can perform any required skills. If not, the candidate cannot be considered for the role.

If they can perform the required skill(s), then the telephone interview questions advance to specific talent questions. Though I will cover talent-based questions in great detail in the next chapter, be aware that talent questions start to assess the presence of the talents that you identified as critical to the success of the role. The goal is to get the applicant talking about what he/she thinks and how he/she performs at work. Talents are top-of-mind reactions. That means the applicants' first thoughts and comments tell you a great deal about what talents they possess. This will be critical in selecting the right candidates to advance to face-to-face interviews.

The telephone interview must be evaluated. The Fire Up! Process$^{SM}$ presents the Employee/Candidate Evaluation

Matrix to be used both for telephone interview and face-to-face interview. The Employee/Candidate Evaluation Matrix is presented in the supporting worksheets to chapter 6 found on the website www.FireUpYourEmployees.com. Follow the directions on the top of the form to empirically evaluate each telephone interview. I will review the Employee/Candidate Evaluation Matrix in greater detail in chapter 6.

The telephone interview's goal is to narrow the selection process down to spend time face-to-face with only those truly viable candidates. This interview must be short, to the point, and focused on whether to advance a candidate or not. To that end, I offer the following recommendations.

- The telephone interview should not exceed twenty minutes.

- The telephone interview starts with any BFOQ or role qualifying questions.

- The telephone interview should focus on the two or three primary role or performance talents from the Talent Matrix and asks no more than two questions in each.

- Create one skill and one experience question to be used if you have time.

- The Employee/Candidate Evaluation Matrix is used to assess each phone interview.

- Ask the same talent questions and BFOQ questions of each candidate. Your follow-up questions will vary based on the answers you receive from each candidate. It is critical to apply the same talent criteria to all applicants since these criteria are critical for the role.

Now, you have better feel for those who should return to be part of the face-to-face interview. I review the process of a high performance interview in the next chapter.

Time for Practice

From the worksheets you printed for this chapter from the website, access the worksheet marked Step 5. Complete your work on this worksheet. This exercise will ask you to prepare for a phone interview for the role that generated your Talent Matrix. Identify any BFOQ questions. Next, prepare one question for each of your top three talents (based on your ranking on the Talent Matrix), using the General and Specific Talent-Based Interview Questions that can be found by printing the detail pages for chapter 6 from the website. Create one question related to the most important skill and one for the most important experience. This will create your telephone interview questions. Complete this activity before moving on.

I will review the remaining steps of the Hiring Process in the next chapter.

**Fan the embers – A summary and review**

1. The interview process needs to be complete to ensure a successful and bias-free hiring process resulting in hiring the right employee.

2. Step 1 of the progressive interview process is to assess the need to hire. Not all employment vacancies need to be rehired; many times realignment of responsibilities will be the better response. Determine the right response.

3. Step 2 is to create the Talent Matrix. This creates the list of talents, skills, and experience that will encourage an employee's success in the role. The Talent Matrix must be completed before moving on to Step 3.

4. Step 3 starts the search for candidates, first internally, then externally. An internal search is the first approach to show existing employees that growth and opportunities exist. Remember that internal candidates must meet the criteria on the Talent Matrix to be considered for the role. Use the robust sourcing strategy to start to source qualified external candidates.

5. Step 4 is a review of the resume or job application. Though the goal is to assess the resume and application for talents, most continue to be prepared in an experience-based method. The ultimate goal of the application and resume review process is to determine which candidates should be considered for the next step of a telephone interview and which do not meet the basic Talent Matrix criteria. Encourage all applicants to submit talent-based resumes that highlight both talents and experience.

6. Step 5 is to conduct a pre-visit telephone interview. This step is for those candidates who seem to have the potential to fit into the role; the goal is to start to separate the stronger from the weaker candidates and to only spend the valuable face-to-face time with very viable candidates. The starting question for all pre-visit telephone interviews should be with any specific bona fide occupational qualifications such as lifting, driving, or language requirements that, if not in place, would prelude the candidate from being hired. It should be followed by several questions two primary talents required for the role (of the four

you defined on the Talent Matrix). The telephone interview should not exceed twenty minutes.

7. The remaining steps of the eight-step hiring process and the powerful talent-based interview questions will be covered in chapter 6.

"*If you think it is expensive to hire a professional to do the job, wait until you hire an amateur.*"

Red Adair

# Chapter 6

## Find Out What You Need to Know
## The Interview and Talent-Based Questions

**NOTE** Before starting this chapter, go to www.FireUpYourEmployees.com, click on *Beyond the Book*, and print the supporting exercises and worksheets for chapter 6. This text includes the information you need; the website gives you access to the exercises, worksheets, and activities you will need to fully complete this chapter and to advance your learning through practice. This chapter's website resources also include the General and Specific Talent-based Questions to be used in new talent-based interviewing.

In the last chapter, I presented steps one through five of the progressive hiring process; this chapter will complete the process. Review the entire process below to remind yourself of the components that must be addressed to hire effectively.

How to INVITE the Right Employee (a Progressive Hiring Process)

> **Step 1:** Establish and define the need – Clearly define employment or task needs and whether hiring or role realignment is required.

> **Step 2:** Create the Talent Matrix – Create or update the Talent Matrix for each role that clearly defines the required talents and the expected skills and experience.

> **Step 3:** Use the Talent Matrix: Conduct an internal search, then external search – Successful organizations first look within the organization to encourage growth. Remember that the Talent Matrix is still the standard for hiring; if existing employees do not have the

required talents to be successful, then the search moves externally. Once you complete the internal search, conduct an external search to round out the number of candidates or if the internal search did not yield the right candidates.

**Step 4:** Review resumes and job applications – Review to determine first round talent fit. Cover the names to focus on talents not on gender, ethnicity, or any other bias. In today's workforce, the additional benefit of hiring for talent is that it generally brings in a more diverse team of employees. The more diverse, the greater their experiences and the more perspectives they offer to the organization. Select those that fit your need for phone and/or face-to-face follow up.

**Step 5:** Conduct a pre-qualifying, pre-visit telephone interview – Contact the potential candidates to assess the first impressions about talent and fit and to rule out applicants who cannot meet the bona fide occupational qualifications.

**Step 6:** Host a face-to-face interview – Host a face-to-face "investing" interview that has a plan to gather specific information about the candidates' talents, skills, and experience that met bona fide occupational qualifications and responded well in the pre-interview phone call.

**Step 7:** Evaluate the interview candidates – Conduct a review and evaluation process that has input from all of those in the interviewing process. Use the Candidate/ Employee Evaluation Matrix to impartially assess each candidate and to create a bias-free, intellectual hiring approach.

**Step 8:** Candidate selection and final offer – Make a formal selection from all qualified applicants and present a formal written offer of employment.

After completing steps one through five (presented in chapter 5):

- You have a clear understanding of the talent, skills, and experience needed for the role.

- You have searched both internally and externally, generated names, resumes, and job applications.

- You have reviewed resumes and job applications looking for talent and skill matches with your business.

- You have selected the candidates from information on their applications or resumes that may be a match to the role and to the organization.

- You performed a brief telephone interview asking BFOQ and talent questions that corresponded to the talents required in the role. You have kept the interview to twenty minutes and focused on questions that could rule out a candidate.

- You used the Employee/Candidate Evaluation Matrix to evaluate the candidates that were contacted for a telephone interview to determine which should advance to the face-to-face interview.

- You are ready to meet the candidates in a face-to-face interview in order to assess the candidate's talents, skills, and overall fit.

Let's review the remaining steps in the hiring process.

### Step 6 – Host a Face-to-Face Interview.

Before you learn how to set the environment and tone of the interview, stop for a minute and answer the following question:

*From your perspective, what is the real purpose of the interview?*

The best way to prepare for an interview is to be clear about its objective. Consider this:

- Today's economy is an intellectual economy. That means the employee controls how hard he/she works, to what degree he/she contributes, and how long he/she stays with the organization. Intellectual capital is owned by the employee; managers cannot mandate it, they must invite and inspire it. This interview is the time to see what an employee knows because it is in what he/she knows that we find his/her value. If, during the interview, you do not ask questions with the particular focus, you could hire poorly. We noted the cost of a wrong hire is approximately 25 percent to 200 percent of the employee's salary.

- In a service workplace, the employee is the face of the organization to your customers. Employees have greater contact with customers and, therefore, they more significantly influence customers' decisions. The right employee can create significantly better employee/customer relationships. This has been proven to drive customer loyalty and performance, which improves the bottom line.

The goal of the interview is to determine if the candidate will provide the return you need based on your required significant investment in them (benefits, pay, development, education, etc.). It is critical to create an environment that encourages the candidate to talk by asking powerful and meaningful questions. The true goal of the interview is to create an environment and rapport that helps the candidate become comfortable enough to say things he/she would not ordinarily say. Only by hearing the candidate's honest responses will you be able to assess the candidate's fit to the role and the culture.

That being said, let's consider the areas of setting the right environment (physical environment), setting the right tone (attitude), and preparing the right questions as the three areas to properly prepare to host a powerful interview.

Set the right environment (physical environment) – Create the right physical interview environment to encourage open conversation, discussion, and dialog. This setting should be warm, casual, and comfortable. Creating a comfortable and professional environment is what makes the candidate feel important and valued; there are many things you can do in the physical environment to encourage these feelings.

- <u>Be on time</u> – if an interview is scheduled for 8:00 am, be ready for it by 7:45 am.

- <u>Set up the interview location</u> – chairs should be on equal footing with regards to height and location. The candidate and the interviewer should sit next to each other, not on either side of a desk. This creates a more balanced sense of power that encourages a more significant and more honest exchange between parties. The interview is not about impressing the candidate with the interviewer's status or role. Rather, the interview is about connecting with the candidate to know what is true – so that it can be assessed to determine if the candidate is the right fit.

- <u>Stop all interruptions</u> – leave word not to be disturbed, do not answer the phone, answer e-mail, or respond to a beeper (unless any is an emergency or is something that cannot wait). If you expect an interruption that cannot be avoided, identify it as soon as the candidate arrives so that he/she expects it instead of finding it an interruption during the interview process.

- <u>Create a private area</u> – the most significant thing that can happen in an interview is to create a bond or relationship with the candidate. This encourages honesty and completeness in the responses of the candidate (he/she will tell you things he/she would not ordinarily tell others). This can happen only if the environment appears safe enough for the candidate to say what is on his/her mind. That cannot happen if the interview is conducted in public space or is continually interrupted.

- <u>Make the candidate feel important</u> – be sure all who are involved in the interview process greet the candidate warmly and by name. Offer the candidate a soft drink, coffee, or snack, and do not leave the candidate alone for an extended period. Create a package of organization information for the candidate that has his/her name on the cover. Define the interview process (who will the candidate speak to, for how long, and the workplace roles of the interviewers). Define your interview process (types of questions, evaluation process, timing of decision making, etc.) to help the candidate know the process and start to relax.

Things to consider

- What do you think it is like for a candidate to be part of an interview with your organization, team, or department?

- What is it like for an interviewer to be part of the interview process with your organization, team, or department?

- How is the interview space created? How could it be more effective?

- How do you see to it that candidates are relaxed and comfortable? How can you improve this?

- Do you interview across a desk or table? If so, what can you do to eliminate this barrier?

Set the right tone (attitude) – Create the right energy to encourage open conversation, discussion, and dialog. This should be candid, approachable, informal, and sincere. This refers to the intangible environment and personal interactions that the candidate finds when he/she arrives. You need to make the candidate feel comfortable and at ease. Remember how nervous people become at something important, so make the extra effort to do the things that will put the candidate at ease. The more comfortable the candidate feels, the more honest and candid the responses will be. The goal is to find out facts. Let the candidate know you are human and sincerely interested in him/her. Take a few minutes to break the ice and establish some common ground. Find common interests (note things from the resume or application).

- <u>Act warm, friendly, and personal</u> – greet timely and energetically upon arrival; be sure the greeting is personalized and sincere. Know some facts about the candidate from his/her resume or application without any prompting. This shows the candidate that you remembered him/her and helps to create a feeling of being important and valued.

- <u>Be casual</u> – have everyone the candidate meets introduce themselves with a first name and ask a non-invasive personal question of the candidate. Also, remember the definition of talents: they are top-of-mind reactions. This means that even when candidates are talking about personal things, you will see their thinking and attitudes (talents) in their responses. Gather information during every moment of the interview.

- <u>Express interest</u> – when the candidate responds or communicates, be sure to listen effectively and with interest. Significant information from the candidate can happen each time she speaks. Staying interested creates a positive, caring tone, and encourages the candidate to continue speaking. Keep the topic focused, but encourage the candidate to keep speaking and adding details. The more interested you appear, the more the candidate will add details. These details are critical to your success in the hiring decision.

- <u>Properly staff the interview</u> – remember that the goal of the interview is to gather enough of the right information to be able to make a sound and quality hiring decision. In order to have enough information, ensure that others are involved in the interview process. (Set up interviews with several employees during the same day to minimize the inconvenience to the candidate.) Use the Talent Matrix and decide on which talent questions each member of the interviewing team will ask. This shows a more professional side as the same questions are not asked by several interviewers. This also allows several questions for each talent assessed and a diverse set of opinions about candidate fit based on the answers. Remember that all employees participating on the interview team must understand the Talent Matrix, talents, and requirement that the interview be bias-free and fairly conducted. Training of all interview team members is recommended.

(Special note: The goal of the interview is to encourage the applicant to be honest to be able to assess facts, to determine talents and fit. Most times, this will happen only when employees are involved in one-on-one interviews. Many managers and senior managers like to host group interviews and, depending on the motivation, they may be effective. In most cases they are not effective because the candidate feels overwhelmed and is forced to think through responses more carefully, which rules out the important, candid first responses. Unless the role that is being hired needs to consistently handle a stressful environment such as a group interview, there is no reason to host anything but one-on-one interviews. Think of it this way: how would you feel in the environment? If you do not feel valued, supported, and important, you will not respond with the candor and honesty needed to make the interview effective. Then the interview will not provide you with the information you need to make a sound selection.)

Things to Consider

- What is your perspective of hosting an interview? Do you look forward to them or find them an interruption and nuisance?

- How much effort do you make to learn and remember personal details of the candidate to use during the interview? Can you identify five important facts about the candidate without the use of the resume? If not, how can you improve?

- What is your team's attitude about candidates? Are they openly welcomed and treated well? If not, how can it be improved?

- How many people interview a candidate and how do you coordinate the interview process with each? Why is it done this way? How can it be improved?

## Time for Practice

From the worksheets you printed for this chapter from the website, access the worksheet marked Step 6a. Complete your work on this worksheet. This exercise will ask you to evaluate the effectiveness of your interview process (the physical environment and the tone you create). Complete this activity before moving on.

Prepare the right questions – prepare questions based on the talents, role and fit, and use the exact same questions for each candidate. Your greatest resources are your Talent Matrix and powerful talent-based questions. Asking the same questions not only eliminates bias, it allows a fair comparison of responses during the evaluation portion of the interview. Appropriate interview questions may all start the same, but you will find that the follow-up questions, based on the way the candidate answers, will allow each interview to be customized and personal.

It is up to you to ensure the interview stays on track, the right questions are asked, and a positive environment is created to facilitate discussion, honesty, and information sharing. Remember, the interview is as much for the candidate as it is for you. The goal is to be open and honest to ensure that both sides have enough of the right information to make a good decision. Environments that are not up front and honest impede the process of hiring the right employee.

When preparing interview questions, stay focused on the goal of getting the candidates to talk. You want to know what the candidate thinks about all of the areas surrounding the job – you do this by asking powerful and effective questions. Remember the 80/20 rule – speak 20 percent of the time, listen 80 percent of the time. The purpose of the interview is to gather information. And you do this by creating an environment where the candidate is comfortable telling you important information. Listen for top-of-mind perspectives and comments. Listen to not only what is said, but what is intonated (intended) by language and body language.

I stated in chapter 2 that in the course of a day we make twenty thousand three-second decisions. The better you align our candidate to the role, the better decisions that new employee will make each day. If a candidate has time to prepare for an answer, you no longer see his/her natural reaction. That means that though the candidate may have gotten the answer right, it may not be core to the way he/she regularly thinks. That means that many of his/her decisions, when not allowed time to prepare, will be made incorrectly. This possibility requires that questions asked in the interview process be unexpected, talent-based, and clearly articulated. I have included my bank of talent-based questions to assist in your interviewing process in the supporting pages found on the website (www.FireUpYourEmployees.com) for this chapter.

It is also important to know the best environments for each type of question; use these questions to control the interview, drill down for more information, get a yes or no answer, encourage the candidate to talk, or encourage the candidate to express and support an opinion. Consider the following question types (paraphrased from a wide variety of business resources):

- Open-ended – this is a question that encourages discussion of an experience or an opinion. The goal of this kind of question is to get the other party talking. Open-ended questions cannot be answered with a yes or no, but rather need a personal explanation – they generally start with who, what, where, when, why, or how instead of is, are, have, has, do, does, or can. Example: How were you able to make a difference in service responses to customers?

- Close-ended – this is a question that is answered with a yes or no. It does not encourage dialog and should be used when a factual or empirical answer is needed. Close-ended questions generally start with is, are, have, has, do, does, or can, and the questions do not look for additional details. Example: Have you worked with Adobe Photoshop?

- Negative inquiry – this is a question that looks for a selection of one of two possible negative events. Its goal is to encourage discussion about either controversial items or to elicit opinions about events that will affect the candidate's position; it also allows the interviewer to see the candidate's choices relating to difficult issues. Example: I have always felt it is better to cut employee's pay than to lay them off in a recession – what do you think?

- Positive inquiry – using the same format as the negative inquiry, this form of question looks for a selection of one of two possible positive events and the reason for the candidate's thinking. Example: Would you say customer loyalty or employee loyalty is more important?

- Leading – these are questions that are asked to direct the candidate's responses to areas that need additional information or where the interviewer needs to know the candidate's opinion about something. Example: In our organization, we feel it is more important to sell on value than to have the lowest price. How do you feel about that?

- Layering – this type of question refers to drilling down using multiple levels of questions. Successfully achieving the right level of detail to fully understand a candidate's contribution to a project, job, or idea requires at least five levels of questions. Example: Tell me about a time where you handled a difficult customer. How did the situation arise? What were your solutions? What was your team's response? How did the customer respond? What did you learn from the experience?

- Hypothetical – this is posed as a supposition (what if) to find out how the candidate would handle a situation. It forces the candidate to think quickly and on his/her feet. Again, the best determination of talents is the top-of-mind or immediate reactions so that many of your questions should be ones to get the employees to think on the spot. Example: If you were responsible for customer loyalty in the retail environment, what is the most important thing you need to address each day? Why?

## Keep it Legal

In order to comply with hiring and antidiscrimination laws, there are many questions that are prohibited from being asked, as their responses could influence hiring decisions based on race, religion, age, gender, national origin, or disability. In today's complex workplace, with extreme employee supply and skill challenges, all managers should focus on hiring the right talent (thinking) regardless of any other factor (short of compliance with bona fide occupational qualifications related to lifting, licensing, or other requirements). Today, consider all workers in your workplace – because the perfect employee for your role (talents for both job and culture) may reside in a woman, minority, older worker, or disabled. Hire based on talent and take advantage of the diversity that comes with the talents. Hiring a Latino or Italian first for talent, also brings strong family and cultural traditions that can add significant value and life to the workplace. Hiring an older worker with the right talents will also bring wisdom, proven skills, and experience from his/her years in the workforce.

Focus on hiring the right employee with talent-based questions. Concentrate on fit, thinking, talents, and attitude. Then focus on skills and experience. Never focus on gender, age, religion, ethnicity, or disability. As the workforce shrinks, you will need to search for talents in every class of employee. For more information, including prohibited interview questions, go to www.eeoc.gov.

## Powerful Questions

To see the General and Specific Talent-based Interview Questions, access the chapter 6 supporting exercises and worksheets you printed at the beginning of this chapter. You will notice they first present twenty general thinking questions. These make great foundation or conversation-starting questions for any interview. These can then be followed by a series of questions prepared around the terminology and definitions of the sixteen talent topics presented in chapter 2. This structure gives you the ability to see talent-based questions that relate to the specific talents you listed on the Talent Matrix to be used for both the phone and face-to-face interviews. Though you can use these questions directly, consider adding more to customize them to your particular roles and environment.

You will notice the questions not only focus on the targeted talent, but they are also prepared in a variety of questioning styles. Use the content and styles that are most comfortable for you. Stay focused on the talent you are investigating, knowing that if the candidate does show top-of-mind responses in line with the talent, the candidate may be a possible good fit for the role.

The goal is to ask several very powerful questions, listen attentively to the responses, and drill down with customized follow-up questions. This interviewing technique will require you to be fully present and listening. If you are busy scanning your list of additional questions, you will miss the information offered in the candidate's response. Also, ask the exact same question of all candidates (for a particular role), realizing that the way to customize the questions and the interviews is in the follow-up or drill-down questions. By using the same questions for all candidates applying for the same role, you can fairly compare responses between candidates and assess each candidate fairly and without bias.

Again, remember that the goal is to ask meaningful questions (related to a specific talent) that the candidate is unlikely to have prepared for in advance. By asking unpredictable questions, related to the talent area needed, you start to see the candidate's first (and most authentic) thoughts. You are not trying to ask questions to trick or trip candidates; you ask questions that force on-the-spot thinking to see how the candidate truly thinks. Only then can you assess whether the responses indicate talents needed exist or not. This will be critical information to make the best decision to hire the right employee.

## Things to Consider

- How will your candidates respond to talent-based questions?

- Where is the great value in a talent-based question?

- How will you ensure your questions are unpredictable and fairly represent the talent you are looking to prove?

- Why is it so important to have questions that candidates cannot prepare for in advance?

- How many questions, by talent, do you think is reasonable to ask a candidate?

- Should every member of your interviewing team ask the same questions or should each member ask different questions around the same talents?

## Time for Practice

From the worksheets you printed for this chapter from the website, access the worksheet marked Step 6b. Complete your work on this worksheet. This exercise will ask you to use the position for which you created a Talent Matrix and to prepare interview questions as if you were interviewing new candidates for the role. Use the provided Interview Questions Preparation worksheet to record your planned interview questions. Start first with your most important talents (those scoring a five). Locate questions that focus on these talents. Create your own questions if needed. Complete this activity before moving on.

## Build the Interview Team

It is important to gather information about the candidate from several different perspectives. Create an interviewing team from a variety of roles in your organization. Though you may be hiring for an accounting or sales role, it is important to have representation on the interviewing team from other departments. Since this employee will also need to be part of the team, department, or organization, it is valuable to have a variety of perspectives about the candidates.

Team size ideally depends on several things:

- Importance of the hired position.
- Size of the team, department, or organization.
- Visibility of the new position.

There is no specifically required team size other than it is encouraged that an odd number of interviewers participate; this uneven number offers a deciding vote in cases of ties. Three interviewers are frequently recommended as three offer enough review perspectives, do not overwhelm the candidate, and allow the candidate to see a broader selection of the organization's employees and personalities to help with the candidate's assessment of fit. A short, one-person interview may have worked well in the industrial age, but in today's intellectual age, a more significant review of each applicant ensures a better fit and a greater return from the organization's investment in intellectual capital.

Work together as an interviewing team to ensure each interviewer is properly prepared with quality questions. As a team, create the full list of questions that will be asked – focused first on BFOQ, then talents, skills, and experience. Allocate the questions to the team so all questions will be asked and the same question will not be asked by different team members. Though many interviewing teams ask the same questions (to see if the candidate responds in the same way), my experience is that it's perceived by the candidate as poor interview planning. If there is a critical question that may need to be asked in several ways, then consider having two of the interviewing team ask the same question. Otherwise, use the time each interviewer has with the candidate to get the most possible information – this happens more effectively when several questions about a talent are asked instead of just one or two.

Each interviewer should maintain his/her interview notes and be responsible for scoring and evaluating each candidate. These scores will be recorded after each interview on the Employee/Candidate Evaluation Matrix. The Evaluation process follows.

Things to Consider

- What is your organization's current interview process and are others included?

- What criteria do you/should you use to determine who should participate on the interviewing team?

- What training should an interview team member receive to be effective and to feel competent and confident?

- What do you anticipate will be the response of your employees when asked to be part of an interview team?

## Step 7 – Evaluate the Interview Candidates.

During the interview, you received much information about the candidate. With many interviews, candidate's attributes, skills, and experiences soon start to blend – it becomes difficult to remember who responded in which way. Effective note-taking will solve this issue and provide a clear trail after the candidate has left. Be sure the notes taken are legitimate facts and talent or experience observations only; personal biases or discriminatory comments are not only out of place, but are illegal. Let the candidate know you wish to take notes and invite him/her to do the same. In today's competitive workplace, there is no room for biases and discriminatory comments; you must assess each candidate strictly on the criteria created on the Talent Matrix and the Employee/Candidate Evaluation Matrix (see a copy of the Matrix in the supporting exercises and worksheets you printed out at the start of the chapter).

As soon as the interview finishes, the Employee/Candidate Evaluation Matrix must be completed. Each candidate should be evaluated independently of others because the goal is to hire the right employee, not the best of those who interviewed. Each interviewer should have a copy of the Employee/Candidate

Evaluation Matrix that has been completed with the details from the Talent Matrix (talents, skills, and experience and numerical value of each line) and has room for an evaluation. Independently, each interviewer should evaluate each candidate using the instructions on the top of the Employee/Customer Evaluation Matrix. This makes the evaluation and selection process more empirically supported than based on gut feel. All candidates are evaluated on their ability to model the talents, skills, and experience needed in the role and all candidates are subjected to the same criteria; these scores are recorded on the Employee/Candidate Evaluation Matrix.

Some teams prefer to complete all interviews, then assemble and discuss. The challenge with this method is that many interviewers start to confuse comments and perspectives about the candidates. If the interview team intends to review the candidates after all candidate interviews are completed, then each interviewer should evaluate each candidate at the end of his/her interview. When all interviews are completed, each interviewer can bring his/her notes and Evaluation Matrix scoring and review them collectively.

Some organizations prefer to assemble after each candidate's interview (again, complete the Employee/Candidate Evaluation Matrix before assembling). Either way, the goal is to independently assess the candidates on talent-based questions, evaluate the presence and degree of required talents, and discuss observations and perceptions that follow the list on the Talent Matrix. Either method can be successful if the evaluation process is completed initially and independently by the interviewer, and then reviewed collectively.

Once discussions and the evaluations are completed, tabulate scores. Multiply the evaluation score times the value score of the talent, skill, or experience. Place this total to the right of the attribute box. Add the column down to calculate the total score for the candidate. This process is designed to give you a more empirical approach to hiring. Be aware that though you may have the top scorer from the interviews, you may still not be satisfied with the score; the response is then to go back to your sourcing strategy and reopen the application process. Always fight the urge to select the best of the worst. Be convinced that your selection is an employee worth investing in.

## Time for Practice

From the worksheets you printed for this chapter from the website, access the exercise labeled Step 7. This exercise will ask you to review the Employee/Candidate Evaluation Matrix to be comfortable using the worksheet to tabulate and evaluate candidates. Determine how you will use this evaluation matrix in your next interview process. Complete this activity before moving on.

## Step 8 – Candidate Selection and Final Offer.

After evaluating the candidates from the face-to-face interview, you are now ready to make an offer to your first choice candidate. I recommend you identify your top three choices. Because the workplace is extremely competitive, you should make your best and most fair offer to your first choice. All offers should be presented in writing to confirm the full terms of employment. Though a preliminary offer notice may be sent via e-mail or conveyed via phone, the final offer letter must be in formal hard copy and should document everything that is negotiable:

- Compensation
- Benefits
- Vacation
- Bonus or incentives

- Position and title

- Starting date

- Relocation or other specific responses

- Other company policy benefits or compensations

Present your offer to your first choice before informing your second or third choices in the event that your first choice does not accept your offer.

It may happen that at the end of the hiring process, no clear candidate option presents itself. At that point, the hiring process must be restarted. Frequently, by redefining the position, a new focus and clearer expectations are established. Consider alternate external sources if previous attempts have failed. This is the time a powerful and robust sourcing strategy will pay for itself. Once your primary candidate has accepted the role, quickly send letters to all other candidates indicating the position has been filled and the information from these candidates will be maintained and assessed for other organizational opportunities. If the candidates were able to advance to your face-to-face interview process, they are viable candidates for your organization. Be sure other departments or teams have access to the application information from those who did not receive the job offer in case those not given an offer may be a better fit in another of the organization's roles. Your prompt and professional contact with each of these finalists will be important and can encourage them to remain part of your pipeline of potential talent.

## Things to Consider

- What is the best method to contact a candidate to convey your initial commitment to him/her about employment?

- What is your organization's policy about contacting candidates for employment?

- What is the best way to contact those candidates who did not receive an employment offer from you?

- How do you professionally decline a candidate and continue to keep him/her in your talent pipeline?

**Fan the embers – A summary and review**

1. Selecting the right employee is one of the most important things you can do to manage your intellectual and human capital. A sound hiring process starts your new focus on millennial management as you cannot allow employees to step up and own their work if you do not hire them into roles that match their thinking. Our movement from the industrial age to the intellectual age has created knowledge workers; employees' value is based on what they know and how they use what they know to advance service and drive performance. Once you invest in the right employee, you have the ability of encouraging and engaging this employee because he/she is already interested and excited about the work – it matches his/her thinking. You can then build a strong manager/employee rapport, which is the foundation of yet more significant performance.

2. To find the right employee, review the eight-step hiring process:

   - Step one is to assess the need to hire. Not all employment vacancies need to be rehired; many times realignment of responsibilities will be the better response.

   - Step two is to create the Talent Matrix. This creates the list of talents, skills, and experience that will encourage an employee's success in the role. The Talent Matrix must be completed before moving on to step three.

   - Step three starts the search for candidates internally, then externally. An internal search is the first approach to show existing employees that growth and opportunities exist. Remember that internal candidates must meet the criteria on the Talent Matrix to be considered for the role. Use the robust sourcing strategy to start to source qualified external candidates. The best option is a blend of internal and external candidates.

- <u>Step four is a review of the resume or job application.</u> Though the goal is to assess the resume and application for talents, most continue to be prepared in an experience-based method. The ultimate goal of the application and resume review process is to determine which candidates should be considered for the next step of a phone interview and which do not meet the basic Talent Matrix criteria. Encourage all applicants to submit talent-based resumes that highly both talents and experience.

- <u>Step five is to conduct a pre-visit telephone interview.</u> This step is for those candidates who seem a potentially good fit for the role; the goal is to start to separate stronger from weaker candidates and to only spend the valuable face-to-face time with very viable candidates.

- <u>Step six is the interview.</u> This includes creating the physical and emotional environments to make the candidate feel comfortable to be honest and open in his/her responses. There are seven types of interview questions that the interviewer has at his/her disposal. Use talent-based questions first; the power in these questions is that they are created around required role talents and they evoke a top-of-mind response because they are non-standard, non-predictable questions (candidates cannot prepare for them). Interviews should be hosted by teams to gather a variety of perspectives about the candidates; the most effective interviews are those with one interviewer at a time.

- <u>Step seven is the evaluation of the candidates.</u> Using the Employee/Candidate Evaluation Matrix, evaluate each candidate immediately after the interview. Assemble as a team either after each candidate or after the entire interviewing process is complete. Use the scoring on the Employee/Candidate Evaluation Matrix to empirically evaluate each candidate on the captions identified on the Talent Matrix.

- <u>Step eight is the selection and offer.</u> Using the scoring on the Employee/Candidate Evaluation Matrix, identify the top three candidates. Contact the top choice via phone or e-mail with your decision and an overview of the offer. Confirm all offer components in a letter. Once accepted, send letters to all other candidates informing them of the selection of another.

- If the process does not generate the right employee, then it is important to restart this process. Do not hire the wrong employee because your best candidates did not accept your offer. Realize that as competition gets more significant for the talent that is in the market, you will see that the employee-focused culture consistently attracts the better candidates, and they are more likely to accept employment offers.

*"They may forget what you said, but they will never forget how you made them feel."*

Carl W. Buechner

# Chapter 7

## You Hired the Best
## Create a Powerful
## On-boarding Process to
## Hook Your New Employee

**NOTE** Before starting this chapter, go to www.FireUpYourEmployees.com, click on *Beyond the Book*, and print the supporting exercises and worksheets for chapter 7. This text includes the information you need; the website gives you access to the exercises, worksheets, and activities you will need to fully complete this chapter and to advance your learning through practice.

You have seen and practiced with the complete hiring process and now have hired an employee who met the criteria you established on the Talent Matrix. You used bona fide occupational qualification questions to ensure the candidate qualified for the role; additionally, you asked powerful talent-based questions that supported the talents needed in the role. You were impressed with the answers from the candidate to whom you made the offer. And you were pleased to see your offer was accepted. Your new employee will now start at the beginning of next week. How do you get ready for this new employee? Moreover, what do you need to consider about this employee's first day and week? Why is this so critical – you just spent an extreme amount of time with this candidate through the application, interview, and hiring process?

Here is an alarming statistic: employees who are not actively included (oriented) during their first week are already job hunting within six months. Employees want to feel they also have made the right choice in accepting the role. Employees who are quickly matriculated into the organization in a customized and personal way feel they chose wisely in the interview process. Remember that the interview is a time for both parties to determine the level of fit – talents, goals, directions, and culture. The new employee is watching whether the things he/she thought would be in place (as described in the interview process) do actually exist. It is well known that employees are asked to be on their best behaviors during the interview process. What both parties ideally should do is to be themselves during the entire hiring process; this is the only way to determine a good employee fit once hired. The best interviews open up the organization; this ensures that when the candidate accepts the offer, the environment he/she starts work in is the same environment he/she observed, assessed, and selected. This is the reason to actively engage the new employee in the culture that he/she saw as a candidate as quickly as possible (generally in the first week) of the new employee start date.

Employees are excited for their new roles. Employees start new jobs with hope, energy, and anticipation of great things. This job opportunity is generally as important to them as it is to the organization. This means several very important things to performance.

- The organization should be equally excited for the new employee, and that excitement should be reflected in the organization's effort, interest, and activities at least for the first week.

- Employees look to start with a significant impact. This means it should be easy for the new employee to succeed in his/her first several projects.

- Employees are excited to be included in and to fit in to their new organization. This means the entire organization should be aware of the new employee and make all efforts to include the new employee in the daily routines to make him/her feel right at home.

- Employees like to feel special. This means that both new and old employees enjoy being the center of attention as they host a lunch, have a role in the on-boarding process, meet the new employee's family, and involve the new employee in the social aspects of the organization.

## What is On-boarding?

What used to be blandly known as orientation has been developed into something far more comprehensive, engaging, and more focused on its goal of dynamically welcoming employees quickly, personally, and completely into the organization. Employees are an investment in the intellectual capital of the organization. Finding and hiring the right employee is not an easy task, so when the process has been done and done well, the welcoming of this new asset to the organization should be a reason to celebrate. On-boarding is the process to welcome and connect a new employee to the organization in a way that informs, celebrates, and anticipates extraordinary performance.

As a change in perspective, think of the old form of orientation as a boring review of personnel forms, mission statements, and outdated policy manuals. Now, think of on-boarding as high energy, people-focused and inspiring, and committed to helping each employee develop his/her presence, performance, and personal impact. On-boarding is the process to make an emotional and functional connection with the new hire so he/she feels the choice to work for your organization was the right one. This activates a new employee's performance and commitment in a powerful way.

Before offering some of the critical components of a successful on-boarding process, remember that your organization has its unique personality. Consider blending this distinctive personality along with the agenda of the on-boarding process to create a remarkable and unforgettable event for your new employees. With today's power of social connection and networks, organizations that do unusual things for the employees, get noticed quickly. In today's challenging workplace environment with employee and skill shortages and highly disengaged employees, organizations that do dynamic and unusual things to win the hearts and minds of their employees not only get better press, they also attract more interest to the organization. On-boarding is a critical component of the workplace brand.

Successful on-boarding programs focus on the following areas:

- <u>Organization fundamentals</u> – clearly define the mission, values, objectives, and goals of your organization. This encourages all employees to know the direction of the organization and the performance level expected. Most new employees will not know your organization's philosophy, brand, and fundamental perspectives until they are shared with the employees. The on-boarding process is the method to ensure new employees become quickly included in the success areas of the organization. All senior management should schedule time with new employees (a lunch, a meeting, a phone call, or some other contact to introduce themselves), share their perspectives, and start to build a relationship with the new employee. The more employees connect to all levels throughout the organization, the stronger the relationships and loyalty levels become. This connection is a core component of the organization's workplace brand. This is the place to establish a connection to all organization items including forms, rules, policies, ethics, and safety requirements.

- <u>Culture fundamentals</u> – consider associating a new employee with an organization buddy. This buddy helps to ensure that the new employee becomes comfortable with daily life in the organization so the employee quickly feels part of the organization and is ready to contribute as soon as possible. This buddy is paired with the employee for the entire on-boarding period and is there to answer questions, take the new employee to lunch, explain administrative procedures, learn the flow of the workplace, complete all first-week education, and add humanity to the new employee process. Some organizations also assign the new employee a mentor; the role of the mentor is to act as a more senior connection for the employee when the employee has performance-related questions and to discuss larger issues.

- <u>Role fundamentals</u> – clearly define and review the job description, and the expectations of the role; its impact on the culture, performance, and results of the organization; and its connection to other roles. Create dynamic learning materials to help the new employee master fundamentals quickly. This encourages a greater sense of confidence and allows the employee to be more productive. Spend time on the details of the role so the employee fully understands and then has the ability to add his/her personality to the role to make it truly his/hers.

- <u>Life fundamentals</u> – make the employee feel at home by showing him/her where to locate the bathrooms, cafeteria, mailroom, and any other critical need. Review the daily hours, parking, and office protocol. It is disorienting and disengaging for employees to learn the flow of a new facility by themselves.

Customization is the key to great on-boarding. In today's have-it-my-way world, employees appreciate things that are done exclusively for them. Though you must cover all of the required fundamentals – organization, culture, role, and life – employees are impressed and connect more to events that are personalized. Let's say this new employee is an avid sports fan. Consider hosting one of the first-week lunches at a local sports bar; introduce the owner, tell the restaurant the reason for the lunch, and have a congratulatory welcome cake for dessert. If the new employee is an avid learner, buy or borrow three books of authors the new employee mentioned and leave them on the desk, one a day for several days. This shows that the organization listens and cares about what matters to employees.

"One size fits all" on-boarding can work; it can cover the details and ensure new employees know all of the information they need. Or, on-boarding can be customized to be more engaging and dynamic to welcome a key asset to the organization and to start a long-term relationship off well and in a way that gets noticed, remembered, and appreciated. It has been said that the only difference between ordinary and extraordinary is a little extra. Organizations that commit to standing out, getting noticed, and performing in the largest possible way, commit that little extra in events like on-boarding. They are aware that in today's workplace, if you blend, you lose. They, therefore, are committed to making every aspect of the new employee's first week (and ultimately the career) something powerful. They realize that this creates a powerful connection with the employee, and this connection is the key to extraordinary performance and increased loyalty. Besides, creating a more standout workplace is a more engaging, fun, and therefore, inspiring place to work. Workplaces that do extraordinary things create powerful workplace brands that get noticed. On-boarding does not have to be "on-boring."

Many things have changed in the new intellectual or service economy. The greatest thing is that employees know their value and that they control their thinking. They know the best way to perform is to feel a(n) (intellectual) connection to their work and a(n) (emotional) connection to their workplace and managers. They want to see this happen from the first day to confirm they chose wisely in accepting the role. This has prompted many human resource departments to significantly change orientation to a powerful and memorable on-boarding process.

To encourage an easier on-boarding process, refer to the On-boarding Plan – New Employee worksheet included in the exercises and worksheets printed at the beginning of chapter 7 and found on the website www.FireUpYourEmployees.com.

To complete the On-boarding Plan – New Employee worksheet:

- First, send the Talent and Thinking Style Assessment™ to the new employee for completion. Have the employee send the results of the assessment to the new employee's manager.

- Record the new employee's top four talents on the On-boarding Plan.

- Through discussion with the employee and from information identified during the interview, complete the Employee Talents, Values, and Interests worksheet to summarize your understanding of the employee's hobbies, interests, and values. This will be important to provide information that will allow you to personalize the on-boarding process.

- Based on the information you now have about the role and the personality and interests of the employee, develop a first-day and first-week success plan. Brainstorm customized ideas with your team or department. Develop this plan and include all employees in its implementation. This encourages a greater connection between the new employees and others and builds a more unified and collaborative team or department.

- Assign a mentor and/or employee buddy to this employee. Define and review the role of the buddy and be sure the buddy has been trained, has the resources and the information needed to be effective. Share the identification of the buddy and key buddy information with the new employee as part of the employment letter. This gives the new employee a contact person for questions as well as creates a personal connection to the organization before the new start date. Also, define the role of the buddy for the new employee; this will guide the new employee's expectations of the role of the buddy and help the new employee use the role effectively before starting and during the on-boarding process.

It is up to you to create a meaningful, engaging, and personalized on-boarding process. This impact will be to empower the new employee and help him/her feel that the acceptance of the role was a wise decision.

Things to Consider

- What is the personality of your team, department, or organization that should come through in your on-boarding process?

- What do you anticipate will be the response of employees who are asked to become new employee buddies?

- What training will buddies need to be effective, and how will you determine who should be a buddy for which new employee?

- How should you integrate your on-boarding process with other departments?

- What are the organization's current orientation or on-boarding procedures and are they effective? How can you change those that are ineffective?

- What do other organizations do to stand out in the minds of their new employees?

- Why should on-boarding be a celebration?

Time for Practice

Identify your most recently hired employee. From the worksheets you printed for this chapter from the website, find the page titled On-boarding Plan Questions. Answer these. Once completed, review and complete the Employee Talents, Values, and Interests and On-boarding Plan – New Employee worksheets to create a more powerful on-boarding process for the employee who was recently hired. Compare what you now have created to what was originally hosted for the new employee. Add your action items to your Action Plan. Complete this activity before moving on.

**Fan the embers – a summary and review**

1. On-boarding is a more updated and dynamic version of new employee orientation.

2. On-boarding programs look to make an emotional and functional connection with each new employee.

3. On-boarding programs address organizational fundamentals, including the organization's mission, vision, values, procedures, policies, and other critical information.

4. On-boarding programs address cultural fundamentals, including integrating new employees into the working culture with the help of buddies or mentors.

5. On-boarding programs address role fundamentals by defining the performance and contribution expectations of the role. This encourages greater employee owner-thinking and an immediate relationship between the new employee and his/her manager.

6. On-boarding programs address life fundamentals by helping employees learn the day-to-day rules, policies, and routines of the organization.

7. Customize and personalize the on-boarding process for employees. Have fun and celebrate since hiring is the process to bring the best employees into the organization. These employees are now the intellectual capital of the organization and will drive results and performance. Commit to adding to your workplace brand by the uniqueness of your on-boarding process and make it an event to remember.

# Section 2

## INCITE
## Employee
## Performance

*Millennial managers INCITE performance when they customize employees' roles and create performance expectations. This customization encourages employees to think and act like owners and connects employees emotionally to their roles.*

*"The best executive is the one who has the sense enough to pick good men to do what he wants done, and self-restraint enough to keep from meddling with them while they do it."*

Theodore Roosevelt

# Chapter 8

## Activate Owner Thinking
## Customized Roles and
## Performance Expectations

**NOTE** Before starting this chapter, go to www.FireUpYourEmployees.com, click on *Beyond the Book*, and print the supporting exercises and worksheets for chapter 8. This text includes the information you need; the website gives you access to the exercises, worksheets, and activities you will need to fully complete this chapter and to advance your learning through practice.

You want only the best or A-level performers, those employees who make a signficant difference in performance. The selection process is critical; hiring employees who have the right talents INVITES the best person for the role. This also prepares you for the INCITE and IGNITE components of the Fire Up! Process$^{SM}$. If you do not bring in the right employees (those who think in the right way for the role), then you will need to continually watch over them (micromanage) in order to achieve the results you need. However, if properly matched to their role, you can allow the employee more ownership and freedom in the role, since they connect to what needs to be done and how to do it – it matches their thinking.

I am now ready to introduce part two of my Fire Up! Process$^{SM}$: INCITE Employee Performance. This section looks to activate employees and help them think and act like owners. INVITE was about finding and hiring the right employees (connecting them intellectually to their roles). INCITE is about customizing their jobs, creating performance expectations to connect them emotionally to their roles. Chapter 9 will introduce Part three of the Fire Up! Process<sup>SM</sup>: IGNITE employee performance where you spend time with your employees through feedback and development to connect employees emotionally to you, the manager, and to the workplace.

Consider this: studies indicate employees change jobs every eighteen to thirty-six months and will change careers ten or more times during their worklife. However, it is my belief the constant employee movement is more a function of employee mismanagement than of employee restlessness in the workplace. Younger generations do need signficiantly more distractions and energetic work enviroments, but not all younger employees are anxious to change roles with the current frequency. Instead, when given the right responsive workplace, employees from every generation commit to more signficant attendance, passionate performance, and overall loyalty. That proves that you, a successful manager, have the ability to signficantly encourage greater loyalty from employees – if you understand how to attract and retain employees in a millennial work environment. And once this environment is in place, we have the mechanism to provide extraordinary customer service.

Most organizations use standard job descriptions to define employee responsibilities. Since our business world changes so quickly, these standard job descriptions frequently limit employee performance instead of encourage it. To guide you in developing a more nimble and flexible performance system, and one that connects each employee emotionally to their work, review the steps of the INCITE portion of the Fire Up! Process<sup>SM</sup>:

1. Establish and review standard job descriptions to ensure employees are aware of fundamental responsibilities.

2. Add job sculpted responsibilities to customize additional responsibilities in the employee's talent and

interest areas and address business opportunities and issues from the Business Review (Strategic Update).

3. Create specific performance expectations that define what needs to be done but leaves the how to the employee to develop, implement, and achieve.

4. Tie the performance expectations to profitability and performance metrics.

As these steps are completed, they address business issues, ensure all position responsibilities are completed, and customize each role so employees are more engaged and interested. When these steps are combined, you provide a customized and high-energy work environment that appeals to your employees – you enourage them to think and act like owners, and connect them emotionally to their work. This is how to INCITE employee performance.

To begin the INCITE component of the Fire Up! Process[SM], we first focus on the business review. This is to ensure that as new employees are added or existing employees are moved, you fully understand and constantly match the needs of the business with the talents and interests of the team.

## The Business Review (Strategic Update) Process

Locate the Business Review (Strategic Update) worksheets in the materials printed for this chapter from the website. Using the worksheets, review the impact of economy, manpower, competition, pricing, funding, or other factors affecting the external environment. The more you know about your world, the more you can lead and guide your employees to respond and be successful, and to anticipate influences on your business. Seeing a new trend will inform the savvy manager about the need to develop employees in new areas to proactively respond. And as you are working on ways of connecting employees more powerfully to their roles, you must know of events that will impact the business and how to activate your employees' talents to respond. The Business Review (Strategic Update) worksheets should be completed at minium every quarter; monthly, if the pace of change requires it.

Next, still working from the Business Review (Strategic Update) worksheets, and from the information gathered, identify any new or modified business opportunities. These opportunities may be changes in services, products, locations, responses to competition, pricing, or other events. Record all of your ideas and thoughts; the goal is to create a list of things to consider. Without a recurring process to review business opportunities, employees will not be ready to push these opportunities into results for the organization or to own them as part of their roles.

Finally, review issues, events, or activities in the workplace (for the organization) that are needed but have not yet been completed. This can include markets that have not been developed, surveys that have been planned but not yet completed, initiatives that have not been started – the things you know must get done but have not yet been completed. Most of us have lists of projects we know would make a difference to the organization if completed but never quite seem to have the time. Recording these events on this Business Review (Strategic Update) keeps you aware of these issues so they can be considered when creating customized components of employees' roles and in discussions of their development and careers.

Now that a review of the environment, opportunities, and uncompleted projects is completed, summarize the five most significant issues, challenges, or opportunities that your organization faces. This is the list that you must address with the talents we find in your workplace (or identify the need to source missing talents). Now that you have this list, complete the final section that looks to define the talents, skills, and resources present in the workplace that can address these issues, challenges, and opportunities. You now have a punch list of critical business issues and the opportunity to sculpt your employees' roles around these needs and their talents and skills. This blending not only addresses core business issues but also INCITES employee performance as they connect to roles that are in line with their thinking AND make a significant difference in the organization.

## Time for Practice

From the worksheets you printed for this chapter from the website, complete the Business Review (Strategic Update) for your team, department, or organization. Complete this activity before moving on.

## Job Sculpting

With this critical information, you now are ready to address the concept of job customization known as job sculpting. All employees want to work in areas that appeal to them. As you start the process of connecting your employee to his/her work, review the Talents, Interests, and Values worksheet. (Ensure that you have the worksheet completed on each employee. Review the worksheet as part of the pages printed from the website for this chapter.) As you better understand your employees and your current business environment, you will be able to identify particular high value tasks that both need to be done and are in line with the interests of your employees. Job sculpting is the process to add responsibilities to standard job descriptions resulting in customized roles for each employee. This customization connects employees emotionally to their work; it engages employees and responds to the organization's strategic needs. Once job sculpting has been done, you will be able to create meaningful and empowering employee performance expectations.

Let's start this focus on job sculpting with a look at standard job descriptions. Job descriptions provide a great fundamental value and should be the first step in helping employees fully understand their roles and required performance. Standard job descriptions can be very effective for the following reasons.

- They focus on training for critical and fundamental skills needed to effective in each role. This allows all employees to develop stronger skills in areas that help their performance.

- They allocate the job tasks evenly to ensure that no employee's position is disproportionately complex or time consuming. This helps employees to feel their jobs are fair and take into account their lives outside of work.

- They try to standardize repetitive functions so as employees change roles, new employees can advance through the learning curve quickly to be effective and contributing.

- In the aggregate, they ensure the responsibility for all critical functions in the organization is assigned and these functions will be completed.

To make standard job descriptions more empowering and more customized, job sculpting can be added. Though the employee is still responsible for all of the standard job description components, his/her role is continually customized by adding high-value tasks that appeal to the employees and address business needs and opportunities.

Let's review several examples.

- You have a sales associate who has the responsibility to connect with customers and professionally handle sales transactions (job description). She also has the ability and interest in gathering information about the buying trends of customers. A sculpted component of her role may be to design a customer survey, gather the information, summarize it, and re-merchandise a retail location based on the results. Though this may not be part of the standard job description of a sales associate, it may be exactly the right sculpted job component for this employee – and it would benefit the business.

- You have a sales manager who is great at building lifetime relationships with customers and inspiring his sales team to perform (job description). He also is a great educator and can easily present and explain information. A sculpted component of his role may be to create a sales curriculum, product education seminar, or a program on negotiations, and teach this subject to the appropriate personnel throughout the organization. Though it may not be part of the role of a sales manager, it may be exactly the right sculpted job component for this employee – and it would benefit the business.

- You have a delivery employee who has an excellent driving record, great rapport with customers, and knows the laws and regulations governing interstate commerce (job description). He is also interested in working on repackaging products so they ride and look better and in spending time with younger drivers in a peer mentoring role. A sculpted component of this role may be to spend one afternoon a week with the production and shipping teams to redesign packaging. It also may include the creation of a peer mentoring program that starts first in shipping and then includes other departments. Though it may not be part of the role of a delivery person, it may be exactly the right sculpted job component for this employee – and it would benefit the business.

Review the Job Sculpting worksheets and the Employee Talents, Values, and Interests worksheet included with the materials printed for this chapter from the website.

## The Job Sculpting Process

This is the overview of how to job sculpt.

Select a role from the organization. Using the Job Sculpting worksheet that you printed for this chapter from website (www .FireUpYourEmployees.com), list the role's most significant job description components; this confirms the role's responsibilities. Next, review the employee's talents, interests, and values from the worksheet of the same name. Compare what the employees is engaged by and interested in to the business needs identified in the Business Review (Strategic Update). Brainstorm with the employee any options that INCITE or activate the employee and address a business issue or opportunity. Record all of your ideas for consideration. Circle several of the ideas that are most important, most appealing, and can create the most impact. Create no more than four tasks or new responsibilities that will be added to the employee's role to create a more customized and sculpted role. Not only will this engage the employee by offering meaningful and exciting performance areas, but it will encourage the employee to step up and own the performance because the employee will create the implementation plan for this new responsibility. Your job as a manager will be to work with the employee to create a meaningful and practical implementation plan, and help the employee achieve the plan.

Reconsider my earlier discussion of the need to treat employees like assets, not expenses. Investing in assets requires time, research, and effort. The process of customizing a job takes time. Next, I'll introduce the process of creating performance expectations – which again takes time. Though the time investment decreases over time, it is still a more significant component of management than before. But, as employees step up, work in their talent areas, and work their performance plans, they need less micromanaging and more feedback, coaching, and development. These will developed in chapters 9 and 10 and will show you how you will have time to help employees perform when you commit to hiring the right ones, set them up with clear expectations, customize their roles, and provide the opportunity for them to own their performance. In exchange for this significant investment in each employee, employees now perform at exceptional levels, own their performance, and remain with organizations for greater periods.

The goal of the INCITE component of the Fire Up! Process$^{SM}$ is to see that the more an employee has a customized performance role, the more the employee connects emotionally to the role. In the INVITE section, you connected the employee intellectually to the role by matching it to his/her thinking and talents. Intellectual connection is important but it is only a portion of what it takes to be successful. Couple this intellectual connection to the role, with a powerful emotional connection to the role, and employees are significantly more engaged in their performance. The final component in chapters 9 and 10 will be to show how to connect employees emotionally to you, their managers. When all three forms of connection are in place, employees are engaged, and they perform at exceptional levels; they are more loyal. This is the key to managing in an intellectual workplace.

## Things to Consider

- What is the most significant benefit of job sculpting for your organization?

- What can be the most significant benefit of job sculpting for your employees?

- What do you anticipate the response of your employees to be when you start job sculpting with them?

- Will your employees perceive it as more work or as an exciting opportunity to work in areas they love? How can you influence this perspective?

- How can your employees help you create and update the Business Review?

- Do you have open and honest discussions about the factors that affect the business and the contributions employees make in the workplace? If not, why not?

Time for Practice

From the worksheets you printed for this chapter from the website, access the Employee Talents, Values, and Interests worksheet and the Job Sculpting worksheets. Select one of your current employees. Be sure you have an Employee Talents, Values, and Interests worksheet completed or updated for this employee. Next, update your Business Review (Strategic Update). Now complete the Job Sculpting worksheet for this employee; ensure that your sculpted options match your business needs with the talents and skills of the employee. Brainstorm options with the employee if possible. Create one or two customized or sculpted job components. Complete this activity before moving on. We will use this information next to create performance expectations.

## Performance Expectations

Our final step in the INCITE Employee Performance component of the Fire Up! Process<sup>SM</sup> introduces performance expectations. For intellectual-age employees to be successful, they must be clearly know and understand their performance expectations. These are the tangible performance requirements that are defined by management, but the process to achieve them remains the responsibility of the employee. Think of it as defining what must be done in the role; the employee will be allowed to create the how to do it.

Employees choose to perform or not. As I presented in the discussion about intellectual capital, it is the employee's choice to fully participate intellectually or not; they own their brainpower. You INVITE their performance and contribution by developing a powerful workplace culture, hire them for the right job, and now INCITE them to perform by customizing their jobs (activating their emotions about work) and clearly defining performance expectations that allows them to have a voice in how they do their work. This is a critical difference from command-and-control management. Today's form of engage-and-inspire management realizes that for an employee to think and act like an owner, he/she must, in fact, be allowed to own his/her performance. When managers dictate both the what and the how of performance, they create blindly compliant employees. In today's quickly changing workplace, you need committed, not compliant, employees. You need employees who understand what should be done, and because they have the right combination of talents, they can create a meaningful way to achieve it without your recurring fundamental daily instruction.

My perspective is the more managers tell employees what to do, the less these managers activate the thinking of their employees. Successful managers clearly define expectations, then allow employees to have a voice in determining how to achieve the expectations; this activates employee thinking. Many managers, however, still have the perspective they must tell employees what and how to do their jobs, and not allow them the freedom to own their performance. This happens because managers either mistrust that employees will deliver the results or feel that they will lose control as a manager. However, when the right (talented) employees are hired and are guided by clear performance expectations, employees actively contribute, perform, and take ownership for their work. Successful managers clearly define their expectations then allow employees to build the action plan to achieve their expectations and to own their work.

There are two primary situations that preclude managers from giving more control to employees; these situations relate to safety or accuracy. These are situations or responsibilities that require managers to mandate the steps of performance instead of leaving the performance steps up to the creative plans of employees. Procedural compliance in aspects of hiring, shipping, health and safety, laws, or financial accuracy generally are not the areas for creative responses. These areas are intended to be supported by standard job descriptions or organizational policies. Performance expectations are for areas where employees have the freedom to choose the process of task or role completion. So as you start the process of creating performance expectations, you will need to identify safety and accuracy job components and mandate their performance steps. All other components can allow employees to have more input in determining how to achieve their performance objectives.

Before the performance expectation process is presented, remember that you, as manager, still retain control over this process. As employees propose action plans to achieve their performance expectations, they review them with you. You maintain approval or veto authority. You have the ability of revising plans, changing steps, and influencing the process. However, the more you allow your employees to create and direct their implementation plans, the more they own them. You will also notice that as your employees develop the confidence to create powerful implementation plans, your role in these plans will move more to monitoring and coaching. Until employees feel confident and see they do indeed have the ability to create the implementation plan (which may be contrary to the current organizational culture), you will need to help them through the process.

The final component in this discussion of successful performance expectations is to include a financial metric. Performance expectations define the standard job description or sculpted job task when done well. For a retail store manager, a performance expectation may be to create a customer-friendly store that is personal, easy to navigate, and high energy. You first notice this is an expectation that does not need mandated steps of performance; the employee can have great autonomy in creating this outcome. Though this is better than a standard job description, it is not as powerful as it could be. To add greater impact to the performance expectation, link the expectation to a financial metric, such as, create a customer-friendly store that is personal, easy to navigate, and high energy that increases sales of Product XYZ by 3 percent over the next three months (or achieves a customer satisfaction survey rating of 4.5 out of 5 over the next three months). Now, as the employee executes his/her implementation plan, he/she is also driving the bottom line or satisfaction initiative. This realization now ensures that all employees have a more significant role in driving, contributing to, and owning results, which significantly impacts owner-thinking.

Examples of financial metrics that can be linked to the performance expectation could be:

- Grow sales of a particular product by ___ percent through merchandising the product based on store demographics. The employee would be responsible to develop the approach for the merchandising where the ultimate goal and its measurement of success would be a certain percentage increase in sales of a product, product caption, or overall location.

- Improve customer satisfaction rates by _____ percent as summarized by responses in a customer survey. The employee would be responsible for perhaps training all service employees in more dynamic service methods that would result in increased customer loyalty or by a particular score (or higher) on a customer survey.
- Create a plan to grow ancillary or complementary products that support a major merchandising line or product by $_____. Do this by selecting the complementary products, merchandising them, and assessing customer reactions.
- Reduce overtime (or total wages) in a particular department by $_____ by a review of staffing roles, manpower, and hours.
- Reduce employee sick time _____ percent by creating a wellness program and a life balance program.

Let's review the steps to complete the performance expectation process.

To create a powerful performance expectation, I recommend starting with a review of standard job descriptions and any added job sculpted tasks; this creates the population of responsibilities that can be considered for performance expectations. Select any of the responsibilities that do not require safety or accuracy – these are capable of having employees invent implementation plans and do not require management to mandate the performance steps.

Let's check back on the retail store manager we mentioned earlier. One of his/her standard job descriptions is to "hire, schedule, and manage the staffing for the location." A performance expectation starts with the job description or job sculpted task, then focuses on the outcome. Let's see the basic job description transformed into a complete performance expectation:

Ensure a highly competent, well trained, and adequate supply of retail sales employees that reduces overtime expense by 3 percent over the next six months.

Now, in addition to knowing what is expected, the employee also has financial targets that, when achieved, drive the organization's results.

Once the performance expectation is established, we review of the talents and skills required by the employee to achieve the expectation. Any missing employee skills (things that can be taught) need to be addressed; missing talents indicate that the wrong employee may be in this role. Remember, I said that if the wrong employee (one who does not have the talents for the role) is in charge of this performance expectation, he/she will not be able to develop a suitable achievement plan – it is not in his/her talent area. If the employee is missing skills to implement this expectation, you define the missing skills and create a plan for the employee to acquire the skills. In this example, the employee may need to learn about hiring for talents, talent-based interviewing, and creating a powerful employee-focused workplace culture. Once the skills have been achieved, the employee is ready to continue creating the performance expectation plan.

Next, the employee identifies implementation plan ideas to achieve the performance expectation. This may require the employee to do some research, investigate options, or confer with others. When ready, the employee presents the implementation plan options to you. You and the employee, together, discuss the plan options and collectively decide on the right approach, define reporting and performance targets and the role you will have in managing and monitory the process. Though it is important to allow the employee to invent and own the achievement plan, it is still critical the plan be successful. This will requires a formal review and management process.

Here are some tips in creating successful performance expectation plans.

- Allow the employee to create the entire plan; if you feel it is incomplete, do not do it for him/her, send him/her back to try again with some instruction in the areas you feel are missing. Be there for guidance, not to do his/her work.

- Define the date the plan is due to you and the areas the plan should cover at an initial meeting.

- Set up dates to review progress and answer questions; this will avoid arriving at the plan due date and having it incomplete or missing key information or having the employee feel overwhelmed by the process of creating a plan. Be sure to go over the components of the plan that you think will need to be present and then allow the employee to fill in the details.

- Require the employee to do his/her research when creating the plan. For instance if the plan addresses the performance expectation of increasing store traffic by 3 percent over the next ninety days, the employee may need to research the cost of new shelves, lighting, signage, or other things that may draw attention to the store. Remind the employee that the solution and steps are his/hers to create.

- Be available for comments, guidance, and support at all points in the creation of the performance expectation plans.

## Measure and Manage

The final component of the performance expectation process is to develop a measurement and management plan. As you allow your employees to do more of their actual work, you actually become more of a reviewer, coach, educator, and even mentor.

Managers now take the time to work on plans with employees, track progress on performance expectations, train, and educate. In the process, employees now advance both performance and results. A significant successful by-product is that employees become more committed and engaged in the process and build a stronger relationship with management. Employees now feel their voices matter, their roles makes a difference, and they see their personal impact on the organization's performance and profitability; they now see the impact of their work. This INCITES true owner thinking, fired up employees, and extraordinary performance. This creates the powerful emotional connection employees need in their roles.

Consider the following tips in managing performance expectation implementation plans.

- Reconfirm plan progress dates. Develop a reporting worksheet that keeps track of plan required dates and progress report dates.

- Define a progress report for the project. Review the progress on a regular basis or at key dates. Depending on the complexity of the plan, some may need frequent review dates and others may need review only when problems are encountered or challenges are experienced.

- Develop an applause response for employees who advance their plans and achieve their expectations.

- Build in time each week to spend time with each employee on some aspect of their plans. It may be in teaching a process, discussing options, traveling to inspect a purchase, directing to others with more information, or any other contact.

When completed, you have a formal performance expectation, tied to a performance metric, an effective implementation plan, and a management plan. This ensures that the performance (standard job description or sculpted task) stays on track and a stronger emotional connection is built between you and the employee. Complete these for all  job description and job sculpted responsibilities that do not require mandated performance steps due to accuracy or safety. This ensures an employee is aware of his/her expectations and has had a voice in the creation of the expectation's implementation plans. This truly encourages a more emotional connection to the employee's job and more owner-thinking.

I recommend you start with several performance objectives that can be easily achieved over a short period of time. This encourages confidence in both you and the employee. The next chapter will introduce the performance feedback process to help you stay in touch with the employee about his/her performance, coach and guide him/her, but hold him/her accountable to the established progress and deadlines. The more the employee sees that he/she is given control and held accountable for performance, the more he/she uses his/her talents in his/her role, feels more engaged, and performs at a significantly greater level. Trusting an employee with greater responsibility can be a difficult thing. It should be done wisely and after a clear assessment of whether the employee has the talents and skills to achieve the performance expectation. Start small; expand as the employee is ready.

At no time in this approach do you lessen your expectations of employees. This is not about coddling employees; employees are fully accountable for their action or inaction, and with the performance expectation process, employees are actually more accountable than before. Extraordinary performance remains your goal. This process encourages employees to step up and act like owners; this process empowers employees to be in charge of their performance and contribution. Each step of the Fire Up!

Process$^{SM}$ is designed to shift responsibility and ownership for performance back to employees. Management becomes more of a coach, mentor, and educator. Today, you must inspire and engage your employees to influence them to fully participate, perform, and make a difference. New methods – new world.

## Things to Consider

- How do you anticipate your employees will feel when given more responsibility in determining how to complete their work?

- How often do you feel you should update your Business Review (Strategic Update)? Why or why not?

- Should employees help you update your Business Review (Strategic Update)?

- What is your greatest fear or apprehension about passing more control to employees?

- How can creating performance expectations that tie to metrics be used to determine how to pay employees?

- What stops employees from thinking and acting like owners?

## Time for Practice

From the worksheets you printed for this chapter from the website, access the Performance Expectation worksheets. Using the employee you selected to complete the job sculpting exercise, review the employee's standard job description, and select one responsibility for which a performance expectation can be created. Complete the Performance Expectation worksheet. Then, select one of the sculpted additional responsibilities for the employee. Create a second Performance Expectation worksheet. Host this with an employee if possible. Complete this activity before moving on.

### Fan the embers – A summary and review

1. Inciting employees is about activating their passions and emotional connection for their work.

2. To INCITE employee performance, start first by completing a Business Review (Strategic Update); this assures you know the issues and opportunities affecting your business. It also allows you to assess your team's talents and skills to know who can help address the issues and opportunities identified on the Business Review (Strategic Update).

3. Review standard job descriptions. Use standard job descriptions for all tasks that involve safety or accuracy – for tasks that require mandating the steps of completion. For other aspects of each employee's role that will use the talents and skills of the employee, set up performance expectations that define their expectations but allow them to develop the implementation plans.

4. Job sculpting is the process of adding responsibilities to employees that both address a business need (or opportunity) and appeal to the talents, interests, and values of the employee. The more an employee's role is customized, the more emotionally connected employees feel to the work. Include no more than four sculpted components to each existing role.

5. Once employee's roles have been customized, it is time to set performance expectations. These define what performance is expected, then allows the employee to define the plan to achieve the expectations. This creates a stronger sense of employee ownership and contribution. Performance expectations can be created for job sculpted

components and for standard job descriptions that do not include safety or accuracy mandates.

6. Allowing employees to have a greater role in how they complete tasks encourages performance so long as the right employee is hired.

7. Management must still be involved in setting the actual performance expectations and the related link to financial measurements with input from the employee.

8. All progress on performance expectations should be summarized regularly; successes must be applauded and sub-standard performance must be coached and counseled. Feedback is critical for all successful implementation of performance expectations.

9. Spend time with each employee to develop meaningful and achievable performance expectation plans. Build relationships with the employees, share meaningful information, and help establish standards for performance that are both fair and include a stretch for growth and performance.

*"You can buy a person's hands but you can't buy his heart. His heart is where his enthusiasm, his loyalty is."*

Stephen Covey

# Section 3

## IGNITE Employee Performance

*Millennial managers IGNITE performance when they create powerful relationships with employees through daily powerful performance feedback and recurring career conversations. This contact connects employees emotionally to their managers.*

*"When teaching, light a fire, don't fill a bucket."*

Dan Snow

# Chapter 9

## Speak to Me About Today
## Using Powerful Performance
## Feedback and Coaching

**NOTE** Before starting this chapter, go to www.FireUpYourEmployees.com, click on *Beyond the Book*, and print the supporting exercises and worksheets for chapter 9. This text includes the information you need; the website gives you access to the exercises, worksheets, and activities you will need to fully complete this chapter and to advance your learning through practice.

I t is time for the final component of the Fire Up! Process$^{SM}$ – IGNITE. To date, you have:

- INVITE – you created a powerful employee-focused culture and learned how to hire the right employee (based on talents) – to connect employees intellectually to their roles.

- INCITE – you have activated employees' performance by job sculpting and creating performance expectations that are tied to financial metrics to encourage employees to think and act like owners – to connect employee emotionally to their roles.

It is time to pull it all together and IGNITE the employee's passion for extraordinary performance. This happens through the emotional connection and relationship built between you, the manager, and the employee through recurring performance feedback and regular Career Conversations (development).

Let's review this critical phrase, "Employees quit people before they quit companies." The converse is also true - employees commit to people before they commit to companies; they just need a reason to commit. Employees respect and connect to their managers when these managers spend time, attention, and effort on employees. There are no stronger bonds for performance and loyalty than the successful employee-manager relationship. And as quickly as people seem to quit people, they also remain loyal to people – when justified.

In the book *Human Sigma*, authors Dr. John H. Fleming and Jim Asplund show that customers become loyal (not just "satisfied") when an emotional connection is created with a company, product, or brand. My experience is this also applies to employees. Employees become loyal (engaged, committed, high-performing) when they not only connect to their work (it matches their thinking), but they also have a personal and emotional connection to their manager. Your connection to your employees by constant encouragement, education, coaching, and feedback builds the important emotional bond. This bond IGNITES performance and encourages loyalty. Let's work on the first step of igniting employee performance through a new and more performance focused feedback process.

## Performance Feedback

Every employee wants and needs a performance status or update; it is a well documented human response to look for the support and approval from another for performance. Studies have shown the most rewarding thing you can do for your employees is to notice quality performance and comment on it – a personal thank you for exceptional performance or a caring and supportive response for problem performance is one of the most powerful forms of employee motivation.

In either case, what matters is your time and effort to inform, applaud, educate, and improve the employee. Savvy managers understand the work environment well enough to know what IGNITES an employee to perform and to become loyal to an organization – and that is to understand and know what value is for each employee.

Although value is unique to each employee, there are three universal performance truths:

1. All people appreciate environments of care, trust, opportunity, and contribution.

2. People want to be treated in the way that they want to be treated. People want to be noticed and appreciated for their individuality and uniqueness.

3. Employees will always want information about their performance to either determine how to improve or to feel appreciated.

One of the best and most effective tools available to management is performance feedback – the process of constantly coaching, educating, monitoring, and evaluating employee performance. This allows a continual flow of information about performance, the opportunity to have a dialog with you, the constant focus on improving, and a strong sense of care and belonging. This is in line with the Fire Up! Process$^{SM}$ of setting performance expectations and performance plans. Employees need constant performance contact as they implement their performance plans and sculpted job components.

Successful performance feedback has rules to ensure its effectiveness because, done poorly, it can do irreparable damage to employee relationships. The most significant asset any organization now has is the intellectual capital (both the mind and the heart) of the employee. The quality of the relationship between management and employee will determine the level of engagement, contribution, and commitment. The more frequently successful feedback is provided, the stronger the bond between you and the employee.

Let's review some of the attributes of successful performance feedback.

- Strong teams need and use successful feedback to keep the team on track and focused on achieving its goals.

- Feedback allows employees the ability to modify their behavior and performance and maintain self-respect, self-esteem, and dignity.

- Successful feedback focuses on behavior and not on personality (the what, not the who).

- Successful feedback provides instruction, not inflammation.

- Successful feedback waits for, or responds at, the teachable (or applauding) moment.

- Successful feedback requires that both parties are good communicators and effective listeners.

- Feedback can be corrective or complimentary.

Each employee is different. That means that though you may introduce and use the same steps to assure your performance feedback is complete, how, where, and when you handle the performance feedback will be dependent on both the situation and the employee. This is the reason it is so critical for you, in today's economy, to get to know your employees. This encourages you to not only place them in the right role, allow them to use their talents, and own their performance, but to understand how to coach and educate them.

*Managers are now like educators; they are the*
*"guide from the side, not the sage on the stage."*

You now see the role of the manager is significantly different from in the past. You now help employees perform by assisting them manage and achieve their performance plans. You will now know early in the process if their implementation plan is reasonable, can be implemented, and the skills needed to implement are resident in the employee. You are still the most important influence on an employee; you are now the coach, educator, and supporter as employees take more and more control over their performance and responsibility for results. An intellectual workplace is built on thinking – employee thinking. Your role now as manager is to IGNITE this thinking so employees perform well, feel competent and confident. As employees expand their contribution and think and act more like owners, you move more to the background. You now ensure that each employee has what he/she needs to build his/her plans and achieve great results.

Some managers feel this focus on soft skills and attention on employees is too coddling and too concerned with how employees feel. Remember, in this intellectual age, how employees feel impacts how they perform – happy employees outperform unhappy employees. This also means the employee must feel important, must always be learning and growing, and must feel connected to his/her work and workplace. The relationship between you and the employee is a core component to creating employee workplace contentment. There is nothing more powerful in millennial performance than the relationship (connection) between the manager and the employee. All other relationships (employee to employee, employee to customer, employee to supplier) will be affected by the employee-manager relationship. Done well, as evidenced by strong, recurring performance feedback, the employee will feel a personal commitment to the manager. This encourages the employee to step up, to perform more significantly, and to work to impress the manager. If the quality of the feedback is average or not productive, this environment can extinguish the flames of any employee passionate about his/her work.

Though this process of performance feedback is not intended to be academic (it needs to be practical), its components must be presented in a structured way to ensure the performance feedback process is complete and successful. This process has three steps; to it I add an opening and closing statement to remind us we are dealing with people and their feelings are important; we must win them in to the feedback. This opening and closing ensures that the employee will not become defensive and, therefore, be able to hear the feedback and be open to its message. All together, it makes an easy to learn, five-step process that works in all situations – home, life, and work. Once you try this, be sure to use it with your teenagers, parents, neighbors, spouse, or partner. It works because it focuses on behaviors, not personalities, and always is focused on performance.

Let's review the Performance Feedback process and then practice to become proficient; refer to the Performance Feedback worksheet included as a part of the worksheets printed from the website at the beginning of this chapter.

> **Step 1:** Start with a cookie (positive comment) – no one likes to feel assaulted with feedback or commentaries about performance – it encourages them to be defensive. Remember that all feedback is about people, behaviors, and emotions. So start each performance feedback with a positive comment, something that shows respect and understanding of who the person is and wins the employee into the discussion. This is critical whether the feedback is to applaud or to educate (improve).

**Step 2:** Describe the current behavior or situation (give great details) – describe what is currently happening, the behavior you want to reinforce or redirect, and the specific situations where you observed the behavior needing feedback. Be specific, brief, and direct. Select the appropriate place to host the feedback (if negative, choose a private place; if positive, a public place may be acceptable). Remember, the goal is to change behavior that needs changing or encourage successful behavior to continue. The only way this can happen is if the event is summarized in enough detail for the employee to corroborate the facts and be ready to continue good behavior or improve bad behavior.

**Step 3:** Describe the impact and consequences (find the hook or the attention-getter for the feedback recipient) – describe the impact and consequences of the current behavior, noting the effect the behavior had on results, customers, or employees. Be specific and quantify details. The more detailed and accurate the information, the more meaningful the feedback will be. This is what is called the hook or the attention-getter. Realize that no adult changes his/her behavior unless he/she sees a personal reason or benefit to change. The impact in this case should not only deal with the organization, but should also be a personal hook for the employee (or feedback recipient).

**Step 4:** Create a plan to continue great behaviors or change negative behaviors (let them have a voice in the response) – work with the employee to both suggest options that would improve a negative event or reinforce a positive event; be sure the employee has a voice in the process, otherwise the implementation of the idea will be ineffective. Remember you are working to encourage employee ownership, so once the employee sees the event and understands, the employee should be responsible for suggestions to correct, improve, or continue. As with performance expectations, the more the employees invent their responses, the more they own the results; the same works with performance feedback.

**Step 5:** End with a cookie (positive comment) – regardless of the content of the performance feedback (positive or negative), employees will process the message better when the performance feedback event both starts and ends on a positive and personal tone. Be sure to reassure the employee of the value of the discussion in the feedback. It sets the stage for an open and honest relationship and dialog about performance. If an employee fears a conversation with you, the concept of successful feedback will be lost. If the employee sees that all feedback is supportive and values the employee, is firm and fair about performance, and focuses on using the feedback to constantly improve, then employees will actively solicit feedback. This way, everyone focuses on improvement; the benefit is greater customer service and organization performance.

Before we begin practicing this process, let's review some of the things we should do, or not do, to ensure consistently effective performance feedback.

## Giving Feedback

Imagine this – Your employee has always done a great job handling problem customers. In fact, you don't know how this employee manages to stay so composed when customers become aggravated and raise their voices. But today, something happened – you are interrupted at your desk by the sound of two very loud and angry voices involved in a bitter disagreement about pricing. You quickly respond and take over the situation and are able to settle the issue with the customer. Now it is time to address feedback with your employee, for we are at the teachable moment. *Stop!* You aren't ready to give this employee any feedback yet – there are several things we need to discuss first. For this feedback to be effective and about performance, we need to remember it must be directed to behavior – go for just the facts. But having just handled this situation, you are emotionally charged. These emotions will override the positive benefits of the feedback if it is not controlled and managed. Anger may be an emotion that can be discussed, but the feedback cannot be done angrily. This is one of the most difficult aspects of effective feedback – emotional intelligence and self-control.

There are many disruptive behaviors that can derail effective feedback. Without control, these disruptive behaviors undermine the feedback process and the benefits of both correcting behavior and building a better relationship with you will be lost. Ensure your success by identifying any of the following behaviors in your feedback style and make modifications where necessary. So before you can deliver effective feedback, you need to manage yourself and your emotions – if you do not, you will create another encounter similar to the one the customer service employee had with the customer. These disruptive behaviors have been adapted and edited from *Coaching Through Effective Feedback* by Paul J. Jerome.

Disruptive Behaviors

*The aggressor:*
Disruptive behavior: Aggressors talk about personality and character traits instead of behaviors. They threaten, embarrass, and respond emotionally and angrily. They use the feedback to vent instead of to teach, educate, or coach.

Examples of the aggressor's comments include:

- "You never think."

- "You are so stupid."

- "You are always so disorganized."

If you see this behavior in you, what can you do to correct it?

### *The yacker:*

Disruptive behavior: Lengthy lectures that move from topic to topic without a clear and concise reason for the feedback. The facts are unclear and are hidden by too many words and frequently too much emotion. There is no opportunity for the feedback recipient to break into the commentary and, therefore, either learn from the event or offer additional facts about the event.

Examples of the yacker's comments include:

- "This is what happened to me when I was starting in a position like yours and even though it is not exactly the same, it is similar enough to tell you this story. When I first started in your position…"

- "Do you know why your response was not okay with the customer? Well, I'll tell you why. Sit there and let me finish."

If you see this behavior in you, what can you do to correct it?

### *The careless:*

Disruptive behavior: The feedback giver is completely inconsiderate of the information or the feelings of the feedback recipient. The careless says what is on his/her mind without regard to audience, time, feelings, or place. This leads to feedback recipient embarrassment, anger, and disrespect for the feedback provider.

Examples of the careless' comments include:

- "Let's discuss it late on Friday so you can have the weekend to think about it" (and get angry).

- "Many of us do not like the way you handle Smith Company" (in front of an office full of people).

- "You still haven't mastered the computer system! My pet gerbil could handle this transaction" (in front of a customer).

If you see this behavior in you, what can you do to correct it?

### *The extremist:*

Disruptive behavior: This feedback giver exaggerates for effect and is famous for using superlatives such as always, never, and every. Facts are not used unless they support the extreme and are frequently ignored. The extremist's feedback comes from an emotional response that uses exaggeration to make a point. There can be no learning from this event since it encourages the feedback receiver to become defensive or disinterested.

Examples of the extremist's comments include:

- "You always come in late."

- "You never have completed anything on time, ever."

- "Every customer has a problem with the way you greet them at the register."

If you see this behavior in you, what can you do to correct it?

### *The negatron:*

Disruptive behavior: This feedback giver sees everything as a negative, generally because of personal experiences or disappointments. This perspective invades the feedback as it finds fault with things and people. All solutions offered have flaws; there are no right answers. This downer personality does not present learning options so, over time, the feedback recipients tune this feedback giver out and the contact is ineffective for either behavior improvement or relationship building.

Examples of the negatron's comments:

- "It will never work – I've seen it all before."

- "You never seem to get it; why are we even trying this with you?"

- "If I tell you a hundred times, you will still never catch on."

If you see this behavior in you, what can you do to correct it?

Emotional self-awareness is a critical component of all great managers. When you understand that all contact with an employee must help the employee learn and build your relationships, you will start to notice aspects of your interactions that get in your way. As you move through the balance of this chapter, commit to noticing your behavior as much as you notice the behavior of your employees. As you learn to use the five-step Performance Feedback process, continue to assess your response, particularly the way you respond emotionally to what you see and experience as a manager.

Remember, all feedback must result in a win-win event; the employee learns and the (employee/manager) relationship improves. Let's pull the performance feedback process together by reviewing a full example. Let's say you overheard your employee Bill on the phone with a customer; Bill raised his voice, was short-tempered, and unhelpful. Here is how the feedback could be presented using the Performance Feedback process to address the issue, act on the teachable moment, offer Bill information, support, and an opportunity to own his performance.

Performance Feedback Process Example:

**Step 1:** Cookie – Bill, you have some of the best customer service skills in the industry. Our customers are always very impressed with our service levels when they deal with you.

**Step 2:** Describe the current behaviors and situations – Bill, I heard you on the phone with Stanton Company. You were short with them, raised your voice, and told them to call back when they knew the part numbers they wanted. You also hung up without saying thank you. Did I hear this correctly? (Give Bill an opportunity to respond.)

**Step 3:** Describe the impact and consequences – Bill, Stanton Company is one of our largest and best customers. They continually send other customers to us, and if we do not treat them with our best and most supportive service, they will not refer others to us. In this competitive environment, we need their support. They were critical in helping us achieve our profit targets, which resulted in bonuses for everyone on the team – including yours. Our relationship with them is critical to our success.

**Step 4:** Identify alternative behaviors – Bill, what do you think you should do with Stanton right now? (Allow Bill to offer ideas and to own the solution). Great, Bill, I like that idea, please get right on it. Mostly remember how important the relationship is with each of our customers. They call us because we know what we are doing and we treat them better than anyone else – it is how we do business.

**Step 5:** Cookie – Bill, you are an important part of the great service this team gives our customers. Thanks for making the difference you do; please keep doing your best to help us be the best in the industry. Thanks.

Start with a cookie – a positive statement. Handle the feedback using the next three steps. The goal is to help the person receiving the feedback own the solution (if something needs correcting) or ways to keep something great going. Then end with another positive comment to reassure the employee and ensure that the relationship was supported in the process. This creates one neat package – performance coaching – sandwiched between two positive statements. This is how to connect with the thinking employee. This is how to encourage the employee to improve, feel supported, and come back stronger. And, in the process, build a stronger trusting relationship with you.

Consider how Bill felt after this event – having been educated instead of reprimanded. This does not mean you can't be or shouldn't be direct and strong with your employees. Powerful feedback is not about dealing timidly with the issues. Instead, it acts as a successful format to deal with any issue, up to and including firing if that is the right response. The goal is to use the format to be complete and develop a rapport with the employee and to improve performance. You don't coddle employees when you respect them as people, value their feelings, and hold them accountable for their actions. Successful feedback must both address performance and relationship building as the same time. This now places additional responsibilities on you to manage your emotions and to stay focused on the value of the employee and the coaching and educating for performance improvement.

Things to consider

- What is your organization's current feedback process? Is your personal feedback process different from the organization's process? Why or why not?

- How do employees respond to your feedback?

- What is the most successful aspect of your feedback? Why?

- What is the least successful aspect of your feedback? Why?

- Do you see any of the disruptive feedback behaviors in your approach to providing feedback?

- What is the value of starting and ending all feedback with a positive comment?

- What do you think about the statement that feedback should be a win-win event – it should provide information and education and build the relationship between the manager and the employee?

- Is it necessary to start and end your feedback process with a positive comment if you are providing positive or applauding feedback? Why or why not?

Time for Practice

From the worksheets you printed for this chapter from the website, access the Feedback Performance worksheets. This practice exercise will provide four employee situations for which you must provide effective feedback. Use the copies of the Performance Feedback worksheet and complete one for each feedback event. Update your Action Plan with action items to improve your feedback performance. Complete this activity before moving on.

### Fan the embers – A summary and review

1. All successful feedback is about performance, not personality; it is about behavior, not character traits.

2. The Performance Feedback process has five steps:

   **Step 1:** Give a cookie (positive comment).

   **Step 2:** Describe the current behaviors and situations (give great details).

   **Step 3:** Describe the impact and consequences (find the hook for the feedback receiver).

   **Step 4:** Create a plan to continue great behaviors and change negative behaviors (let them have a voice in the response).

   **Step 5:** Give a cookie (positive comment).

3. Be aware of any disruptive feedback style you may have; identify when it is happening and create a plan to correct it.

4. Performance feedback is most successful when it is done at the teachable moment – the point when the feedback event took place and the time when the learning from the event will be most effective.

5. Employees must always have a voice in determining a feedback response; this encourages their ownership of the plan to correct a skill or performance shortfall or a process to maintain successful performance.

6. Performance feedback is not limited to performance errors; performance success should also generate performance feedback. Feedback on successful performance encourages the performance.

7. The emotional connection and relationships building that results from the dialog and coaching between employee and manager is what ignites the employee's performance.

# Chapter 10

## Speak to Me About Tomorrow
### Career Conversations and Performance Development

**NOTE** Before starting this chapter, go to www.FireUpYourEmployees.com, click on *Beyond the Book*, and print the supporting exercises and worksheets for chapter 10. This text includes the information you need; the website gives you access to the exercises, worksheets, and activities you will need to fully complete this chapter and to advance your learning through practice.

High performing intellectual-age employees want their work to be a critical component of their lives. That means they have expectations, visions, and plans about what work is and what it will be. Career development is the process of discussing, planning, and acting on steps to advance both the performance and capabilities of each employee.

If an employee is to be fired up – IGNITED to perform – he/she must have a strong connection to you, the manager. This connection and relationship is built by the things I have discussed to date – investing the time to put the employee in the right role based on the employee's interests and talents, spending time creating performance expectations (and letting the employee build a plan to achieve them), and providing daily supportive performance feedback and direction. In each of these steps, you see millennial management is developed through an intellectual and emotional connection with each employee. This requires considerable time and effort; as such, employees are valued as assets. You invest in their intellectual capital, and in exchange for this investment, you look for a significant return.

By completing the steps presented thus far, you and the employee can now have an open and honest relationship that is strong enough to participate in a successful career discussion. A Career Conversation is a recurring dialog about the skills and professional development, advancement, and progress of the employee within the organization. Its goal is to not only create an opportunity to address some of the organization's needs, but also to match these needs with the directions, interests, and talents of the employee.

In the past, a development process was much less important. With a greater number of employees performing similar work processes (manufacturing), the concept and discussion of customizing the role and defining what is next for the employee was not as significant. Today, in our intellectual or service age, what you know is what helps you perform and be the most in demand. You are in the age of free agent thinking; employees feel they must have the best skills to ensure they control their movement to greater performance and, therefore, greater rewards. Employees are now more interested in where they are, where they are going, and what they need to get there. They want this help from you or they will change employers until they find one who thinks this way. Younger generations are well connected to their peers; when they know of an employer who commits the time to build meaningful employee and performance relationships, they tell their friends. Statistics support that word-of-mouth advertising (including telling others how great a workplace is) is fifty times more effective than paid advertising. Employees who love their work, have a great relationship with their manager, and see a viable, meaningful career path, tell their friends and market the organization's workplace brand.

Let's move into the final component of the Fire Up! Process<sup>SM</sup> – the development process that I title Career Conversations.

Many organizations use the word development with a variety of meanings so before I move on, let's define what development is and isn't.

## What Development Is

- Generally: development is the short- and long-term process to expand the performance capacity and capabilities of an employee.

- Specifically: development is:

    —The discussion with you, the manager, to continually investigate ways to better connect the employee's talents to his/her role.

    —The discussion with you to assess and augment the employee's skills and education needed to improve short- and long-term performance.

    —Discussions with you to look to the future for ways to expand the employee's performance, define career directions, build achievement plans, and inspire employee loyalty.

## Things to Consider

- What has been your experience with development or a development process? What was done to match your talents with your current role? What was done to look to the future to help you grow in areas that match your interests, talents, and values?

- If done well, what was done? If not done, why?

- What do you think your current employees want for a development discussion? Why?

- Is development a way to inspire greater loyalty from your employees? Why or why not?

### What Development isn't

Development is not a focus on perpetual promotion. As presented in the late 1970s' book *The Peter Principle* by the business writer Laurence J. Peter, organizations are victims to the hierarchies they create and consistently promote their employee to their level of incompetence. This is because there is continual pressure in most organizations to promote to advance; their hierarchy shows the greater rewards and titles follow the higher movement on the advancement ladder. As a result, most employees see promotion as the primary the way to earn more, receive greater praise, and advance.

As Marcus Buckingham presents in his book with Donald Clifton, *First Break All the Rules*, there is a flaw in conventional thinking about development: in many cases the talents required to be successful in the new and more elevated role may not be similar to the talents needed to excel in the previous role. A promoted stock room employee is not necessarily an effective operations center manager. A promoted facility or store manager is not necessarily an effective sales manager. A promoted local salesman is not necessarily successful in a regional or national supervisory sales role. There are different talents needed to be effective in each role, based on role functions and the organization's culture. As a result, the natural promotion to the next position can become a large performance problem for an employee because if the employee is ineffective or performs poorly in the new role, he/she is now stuck; he/she cannot return to where he/she was, and he/she cannot perform effectively where he/she is. The result is that performance suffers until the employee is either fired or leaves on his/her own.

Development discussions must always include a discussion of talents. Talents, "those recurring patterns of thought, feelings, and behavior that can be productively applied" as defined by

Marcus Buckingham and Donald Clifton, remain at the core of development.

So, here is one of the most challenging management questions: How do you help an employee focus on the future, concentrate on his/her talents, and respond to business needs and opportunities? This is the core of millennial management – connection, fit, and performance. The more employees' growth focuses on their talents and the needs of the business, the greater the organization's results. Provide a growth path for employees and most stay. Ignore this discussion and the employee returns to changing jobs every eighteen to thirty-six months. This is how to end the chronic turnover cycle.

The Career Conversations process has the following four areas:

> **Step 1:** Business Review (Strategic Update): Start with a reconnection to the Business Review (Strategic Update) presented in chapter 8. This provides an updated look at critical issues, challenges, and opportunities facing the business or organization (this will always be the development starting point as development must match employees' talents and future performance with the needs of the organization).

> **Step 2:** Job Sculpt: Next, review the employee's talents, interests, and values to determine if the current role needs sculpting or adjustments to keep the employee engaged in the short term.

> **Step 3:** Career Development: Complete the Career Conversation process using the Career Conversation worksheets. These worksheets develop a one-year and three-year career development plan based on the needs of the organizations and the talents, values, and interests of the employee.

**Step 4:** Succession Planning: Finally, summarize your assessment of the employee and his/her Career Conversation plan for senior management; this assessment informs them of the current and potential future employee bench strength and influences the organization's succession planning process.

## Step 1: Business Review (Strategic Update)

As with the discussion of job sculpting, all development discussions must be framed by an understanding of the needs, challenges, and opportunities of the business. A clear understanding of things that affect the business will help to ensure all employees' programs, development, and advancement will always look to balance the needs of both the employees and the organization. Therefore, all development should start with an update to the Business Review (Strategic Update) presented in chapter 8.

Additionally, starting with a full understanding of the business ensures you have an active role in talent and succession planning by knowing which roles employees can and will be moving to/from in a short- and long-term perspective. As vacancies are created by employee movement, the organization can activate an appropriate robust sourcing strategy to find appropriate replacement candidates – internally or externally. Knowing this early allows the process of finding, interviewing, and selecting the right employee to be effective. The best thing you can do for your employees is to help them continue to grow and develop. Employees want to see a limitless horizon – and have input in determining how to achieve it. They also want to fit into the needs and vision of the business; they want to make a difference. Take this vision away, particularly for the younger generations, and you unintentionally ask your employees to leave.

## Step 2: Job Sculpt

Now that you have updated the organization's critical issues and opportunities, review the particular employee whom you are planning to develop. Be sure an updated Employee Talents, Values, and Interests worksheet has been completed, and based on your regular contact with the employee, assess your answers to the following questions:

1. Is the employee engaged and happy to be in this role?

2. Does this role give the employee an opportunity to do what he/she does best?

3. Has this role been sculpted to make it more customized and more interesting?

4. Does this employee continually contribute his/her best?

If any of these questions result in a no answer, then one of the critical development components will be the need to job sculpt. Refer back to chapter 8 and the job sculpting process. Remember that job sculpting is a current response to engaging an employee; does the job today captivate his/her interests and use his/her talents. A look at today's role is always the starting point for all employee development.

Besides ensuring employees are activated in areas that both affect the organization and match their talents, job sculpting also has a significant role in development. By adding responsibilities to each employee's roles, you can assess the employee's abilities for greater performance and expanded roles. Job sculpting allows managers to see employees' capabilities as new tasks and responsibilities are added to their standard roles. Remember that great employee development has both a skill and career component. Part of the discussion during the Career Conversation process will be to look at current changes to responsibilities to customize employee roles. It will also address advancement in a one- and three-year period as part of its look to the future.

### Step 3: Career Conversations

Once job sculpting has been completed and the employee's current role is customized to activate the employee's talents in areas of particular business needs, you are ready to start to look to the future for this employee. The Career Conversation process discusses both short- and long-term opportunities that appeal to both the organization and the employee. Remember these things as you approach this section:

1.  Employees must advance in areas that match their talents.

2.  Consider employee short- and long-term development as it affects the organization's business review.

3.  Solicit input from employees but remember you have the final word.

At no point in this process is it exclusively about what an employee wants. You are including the employee in the process to encourage dialog and input. There may be times where what employees want and what makes sense for the business do not exactly match. This then informs management of possible employee departures. The goal is not to keep every employee, but to keep those who fit at all levels. Though you should be flexible to keep the great employees by continually job sculpting and creating short- and long-term opportunities that benefit both employee and organization, you are ultimately accountable for the bottom line.

With this thinking, let's prepare to host a regular Career Conversation. Career development is a critical component of all employee-focused cultures (as I covered in chapter 1); it shows the commitment to the employee that management engages in a thoughtful discussion with each employee to determine a practical and personal career development plan. Additionally, it allows a conversation between you and the employee about the employee's development and direction. This conversation is a critical opportunity for an employee to comment and dialog about where the opportunities are, which are matched to his/her talents, and what the future could look like. Most employees leave because of either a conflict with their manager or no clear vision of their career opportunities. This Career Conversation process addresses both, which provides another component of a highly successful employee-focused culture. The Career Conversation represents one of the strongest employee/manager connections possible and is critical to successful millennial management and the Fire Up! Process$^{SM}$.

The Career Conversation process begins with a discussion of the short term; the focus is on the next year. This is done to show employees the development process with a near-end goal. If the goals are too far in the future, employees may lose interest or connection to the role. By creating both a one-year and three-year plan, the employee has more control over the progress and has objectives that are not so distant they seem unachievable or inaccessible.

In order for this process to be effective, it must have the following:

1. Accurate information – (about business needs, employee talents, and skills) – this process relies on information about the organization and the employee; it is only effective when the information is accurate. Gathering information will be through observation and conversations with employees. Use whatever sources are available to gather the best information – about the environment and the employee. Check it before using it.

2. Adequate preparation – as with the hiring process, this process takes time to do it well. A poorly prepared or rushed Career Conversation will either create a poor plan or ensure the employee does not feel valued and important (remember that your employees, not you, decide at what level they'll contribute in the workplace). The initial preparation will require significantly more effort to become familiar with the process and to gather meaningful information. Once completed, to update the information will require considerably less time. This process is an investment in your employees; the return is extraordinary performance.

3. A creative look to the future – invent roles of high professional and organizational value to keep your employee excited and engaged and keep results and performance high. This process requires a non-conventional approach; conventional thinking offers a weak and predictable development response. When you brainstorm with your employees and invent opportunities (by ignoring any restrictions or limitations while inventing responses), you develop more attractive ways to keep employees challenged and engaged.

## Step 4: Succession Planning

The decisions made during the Career Conversation help to shape the future employee talent pool. As you discuss career options and ultimately decide on employee directions, you are now able to pass this information on to senior management. This information now assists in succession planning by understanding which employees are moving to which roles, which may be leaving, and which are able to relocate for opportunities. Organizations need to be well informed of the intentions of its employees. An open and honest dialog that focuses on both the employee's talents, interests, and values and the needs and opportunities of the business provides accurate and highly valuable information for long-term staff development and organization strategic objectives.

The best way to maximize the impact of the Career Conversation for the employee and the organization is to see it as a cohesive process. Here are the steps and guidance to complete a full Career Conversations process (refer to the worksheets printed for this chapter from the website, www.FireUpYourEmployees.com).

## Completion Steps for the Career Conversations Process

1.  Be sure that the Business Review (Strategic Update) has been completed.

2.  Complete the Job Sculpting worksheet for any current job modifications.

3.  Career Conversation (Part 1 – Employee Information) – Much of this information has been completed on the Employee Talents, Interests, and Values worksheet; it is critical to include it here as it sets the stage for a career and performance development discussion. Additionally, this worksheet looks for the employee's least and most favorite aspects of their role. The obvious goal is to see what direction this information can be used to discuss career options. Finally, the worksheet looks at employee skills. This is used to identify what skills are at a successful level and which need improving to be effective at the current or future role. Skills that are insufficient should include an education response in the development action plan. This worksheet is now a summary of how the employee thinks, what the employee knows,

what he/she is good at, and what he/she likes and dislikes about the job. This one page has all the critical information to fairly represent the employee side of the Career Conversation. Couple this with the Business Review (Strategic Update) completed by you, and you have both sides ready to start the process of career and performance development. This worksheet is to be completed by the employee (and/or reviewed by or assisted by the manager).

4.  Career Conversation (Part 2a – Employee Direction) – This worksheet starts the conversation part of the process by documenting the areas the employee wants to be involved in at one year and at three years; this is the employee's vision of the future guided by management through an understanding of his/her talents and performance areas. An honest dialog is required for the employee's career options to be meaningful and based on capabilities. This level of honesty will be critical to create a plan that is meaningful for the employee, work to retain the employee, and act as a sound platform to build an action plan to achieve the career plan.

5.  Career Conversation (Part 2b – Career Options and Plan) – With the information from the Business Review (Strategic Update), a completed employee profile and the employee's list of where he/she would like to be in one year and three years, you now start to consider future opportunities that address both employee and business needs; you have the starting point for a possibilities discussion. Worksheet Part 2b records the options for both job sculpting and career development that are discussed, supported by the information about the business and about the employee. The top of the worksheet records

all of the brainstormed possibilities. Remember – development does not always mean promotion. As I presented in our discussion of talents, one role may not lead to another. The only time promotion should be included is if the talents of the employee will match those needed to perform well in the promoted role.

Do not concentrate on only creating standard policy or common responses. This section requires both parties to be creative about where the employee best fits (even if a role doesn't exist at the moment), blended with the needs of the business. Creative minds impose no limits on inventing options – this is meant to be a creative what if or how about discussion. Create a list of as many options as possible that address both business and employee perspectives. Only once you feel the list is as complete as it can be, start the process of selecting one or two job sculpting options (if needed or not already completed) and two or three career development options to implement. Be sure to get the employee's perspective and agreement because if the employee feels the options were imposed by you, the career development plan will not be successfully implemented.

Once the options are selected, the employee then creates the action plan to implement the job sculpting, short- and long-term plan components. This plan should address the implementation process, additional training, tentative timetables, and other specifics that can be tracked, measured, and managed. Once completed, review the plan and build a management support plan. The management plan must include specific timetables, expectations, and other empirical details to hold both you and the employee accountable for its implementation and tracking. This form is now dated, signed, and can be sent to the human resources department to be included in the employee's personnel records.

6. Career Conversation (Part 3 – Succession Planning) – As part of the development process, you have a very clear understanding of each employee's direction both short- and long-term. You are now able to update senior management by completing a status assessment on each employee. This does two important things:

   • It identifies the Career Conversation has been completed;

   • It identifies for planning and advancement purposes, who is in the pipeline for mobile or local growth, or who needs performance counseling. This addresses the critical brain drain challenge of retiring employees and the potential loss of what they know. By knowing who is capable of moving forward, organizations can start pairing high potential employees and retiring management together to build a strong succession plan, and to understand their bench strength. This also should be conveyed to human resource executives to allow for a more proactive talent recruiting process.

The assessment captions on this worksheet are:

   • High mobile growth – employees who have the interest and ability to progress and are willing and able to relocate for an opportunity if the organization has multiple locations.

- Local professional growth – employees who have the interest and ability to advance to other and more significant positions but are unable or unwilling to relocate.

- Local personal growth – employees who are content with their current position (not looking for position changes or advancement) but are good workers and are willing to continue to grow personally.

- Pending further action – employees who are underperforming and either need counseling to improve performance, a modification of job functions (more in line with employee talents), or need to be counseled out of the organization.

What makes this approach so effective is that it forces both parties to fully understand their environments, talents, and directions. It then assembles both parties to share critical information that benefits both and asks each to invent opportunities that appeal to both. Once a list is proposed, both parties negotiate a direction. Though it is not a commitment to the employee that a particular role will belong to them, it does instead define the direction an employee is headed, allows time to assess if the future role is a fit, and allows the employee time to develop the skills to master the role.

Realize that the goal is to retain the best employees. Note that in a Career Conversation, both you and the employee may become aware the opportunities the employee wants and needs may not be available in the organization. To that point, remember the Peter Principle presented earlier. If the employee is not right for the role and is promoted regardless, it will be only a matter of time before the employee realizes the role is not a good fit and leaves, or the organization sees that work is not done well and asks the employee to leave. Have the courage to deal with fact. If there is a great fit for the employee and the business, then advance the plan. If there is not a great future fit for the employee and the business, assist the employee in finding other opportunities more in line with the employee's talents and career aspirations. The positive marketing earned by this mature response has been proven to help organizations by its goodwill.

The greatest thing to remember is that a manager's role is to look into his/her employees to determine how to release the talents that are present. This may require a different approach with each employee. The Career Conversation worksheets are designed to be flexible for all employees and to be sure all critical areas are addressed during the process. Be sure to customize and invent solutions to keep employees always growing and learning – remember that development does not necessarily mean promotion.

The Career Conversation is critical for all employees. All employees want to know where they are headed, if the destination is in line with what appeals to them, and how long the journey will take. Organizations that do not host conversations about employees' futures will quickly lose employees to organizations that work with employees to achieve their career aspirations. The world has changed and now employees own a more critical component of performance; they have more say in what they do, how they do it, and how long they stay. You know they are having these discussions and conversations with their networks and friends. Be sure you initiate this conversation and show your interest in each as a person, as a value builder and as a future employee.

Things to Consider

- What do you envision will be the most difficult part of hosting a Career Conversation or with an employee? Why? What can you do to solve this or make this easier?

- What would be the impact on your attitude, interest, and engagement level if your manager regularly hosted a development or career discussion with you?

- What do you think your employees will say or think when you introduce this process?

- What do you need to do to ensure the Career Conversation's What value does the Business Review (Strategic Update) provide for this process?

- How will the Career Conversation process influence your organization's succession planning process?

## Time for Practice

From the worksheets you printed for this chapter from the website, access the Business Review (Strategic Update); Job Sculpting; Employee Talents, Values, and Interests; and Career Conversations worksheets. This exercise requires you to complete the full Career Conversations process for one of your employees. First, update your Business Review (Strategic Update) previously completed. Then, for the employee selected, update the Employee Talents, Values, and Interests worksheet. Assess whether job sculpting is needed (to customize the employee's current role) – if so, complete the Job Sculpting worksheet. Once this information is assembled, complete the Career Conversation worksheets. Update the employee information on Part 1. Start a discussion of the employee's interests in a one- and three-year timeframe, and record important points on Part 2a. Decide on which plans will be implemented and complete Part 2b. Share the information about this employee with senior management by the assessment on Part 3. Complete this activity before moving on.

### Fan the embers – a summary and review

1. Career and performance development is the short- and long-term process to expand the performance capacity and capabilities of an employee.

2. Development is not a perpetual focus on promotion.

3. Great development will always address three critical areas:

   a. Job sculpting – creating a customized job fit for today's role.

   b. Career development – with a short-term focus (one year).

   c. Career development – with a long-term focus (three years).

4. All development and job sculpting starts with a Business Review (Strategic Update) to define the challenges, issues, and opportunities of the business. This is a recommended monthly event.

5. Complete the Employee Talents, Values, and Interests worksheet to fully understand each employee.

6. Blend the needs of the business with the talents, interests, and values of the employee to create highly engaging new responsibilities that also respond to business needs – currently with job sculpting and in the future with Career Conversations.

7. Career Conversations should be hosted at least once a year as a formal exercise (more often as the workplace changes) and should be included in the employee's personnel file or folder.

8. The Career Conversation process can support a successful succession planning approach. It

identifies for planning and advancement purposes, who is in the pipeline for mobile or local growth, or who needs additional performance counseling. By knowing who is capable of moving forward, organizations can start pairing high potential employees and retiring management together to build a strong succession planning process and retain great intellectual capital.

# Section 4

## Smoke the Competition

"We are what we repeatedly do; excellence is not an act but a habit."

*Aristotle*

# Chapter 11

## Create a Successful Millennial Manager Role in a Stand Out Organization

**NOTE** Before starting this chapter, go to www.FireUpYourEmployees. com, click on *Beyond the Book*, and print the supporting exercises and worksheets for chapter 11.

### *Pull It All Together*

You have completed the Fire Up! Process[SM] – a new and powerful intellectual-age management process. You INVITED the best employees by creating an employee-focused culture and by learning how to hire employees based on talents; you connected our employees intellectually to their roles. You INCITED employees to own their performance by the customizing each role with job sculpting that takes into account the talents of the employees and the needs of the business. You created performance expectations for each role to define what needed to be done but left how to do it to the employee; you connected your employees emotionally to their roles. You IGNITED your employees by powerful manager/ employee relationships as you learned how to provide consistent performance feedback and career and skill development; you connected your employees emotionally to you, their manager.

This process completely changes how employees are managed. As the industrial age gave way to the intellectual age, our management methods had to change. As Dr. Lois Frankel says in her book *See Jane Lead*, "People don't want to be told what to do, when to do it, and how it should be done. Not only do they not want it, they won't allow it." The focus on strong, centralized, military-based, command-and-control management actually works against performance in today's intellectual workplace. Today, you must inspire and engage employee to activate their performance. Today you must INVITE, INCITE, and IGNITE employee performance, and do this through a new and more powerful millennial management that focuses on the power of connection – intellectual connection of the employee to his/her role and the emotional connection of the employee to his/her team and manager. Performance remains the goal; the method to achieve it has changed.

Employees want to perform; it is frequently your management methods and workplace that inhibit this. Today's problems in performance are more about management than they are about employees. Management methods must be determined based on the particular performance needs of the employees you are managing. Today's workers contribute by thinking. Thinking is personal; humanity has reentered the workplace. This requires a return to soft skills, connection, emotions, and feelings. These are the needs of today's workplace and, therefore, your management style must work to activate them if employees are to perform.

Employees today require greater relationships, connection, input, creativity, inclusion, and freedom. This means that managers must become better communicators, listeners, collaborators, nurturers, and relationship builders. Today's management style must accommodate this, or employees do not respond and performance suffers. Basing management styles on previous practices is a formula for performance disaster. The more flexible and connected you become, the more you can activate the performance levels you need from each employee.

Your Style

Though this is a new world of soft skills, emotional intelligence, and a more humanistic approach to the workplace, it will be up to you to fully define your role and style. The Fire Up! Process$^{SM}$ presents a comprehensive approach and set of tools to manage in today's workplace; it is your choice which of the tools will have the greatest impact with your employees. Remember customization. It is up to you to create your role with the tools in a way that matches your personality, style, and ensures employee effectiveness. Be sure to create your management and workplace brand – one your employees share with their friends and social networks as you and your organization become the manager and workplace of choice.

The Fire Up! tools have been designed to regularly bring you and the employee together in more person-to-person environments. You'll notice that these tools require continual dialog and conversation. These are not tools and worksheets that you complete and employees receive. These are interactive tools that must be used with conversation, discussion, and honesty. The goal is to create trust between you and the employee; this is one of the greatest ways to encourage employee loyalty. This process creates and supports the ability to openly talk, share, invent, try, and consider things that both help the customer and the employee. The easier this process is, the more employees open up, commit, and perform in the workplace. Customizing these tools is your way to make managing your organization unique to you with performance, employees, and results in mind.

These tools may feel a bit odd, unusual, or foreign as you start to implement them. Coming from an era of demanding and dictating, a shift to engaging and inspiring, to focusing on employees' feelings, interests, and talents may feel awkward and counterproductive. But by understanding how the workplace has shifted the definition of performance from hands to head and heart, we see this is the best approach to address performance.

The greatest way to master this process is to practice. I recommend this process be implemented in two ways: short- and long-term. In the short term, identify several of the tools to implement with employees with whom you feel you will have the most positive response and provide the greatest impact on performance. When implementing anything new, always focus on the areas that can yield the greatest immediate success. Find your best performers and start the dialog process about talents, interests, and values. Assess whether your best employees are in the roles that match their talents and be sure to have them complete the Talent and Thinking Style Assessment™. Create a Talent Matrix for their role and determine their best fit. If changes are needed, start small to first test your ideas and to gradually win the employee into the changes. Identify several performance expectations and allow this/these employee(s) to develop their action plans to achieve them. Review the plans with them and determine how you can help manage and monitor their progress. Meet with them regularly to assess their progress and to provide performance feedback. Select one of your most loyal and capable employees and go through the Career Conversation process with him/her. See the impact on this employee. Modify your approach for problems, or expand your approach in success areas.

From a long-term perspective, define the larger changes that are necessary. This is the purpose of the action plan components built at the end of each chapter. Develop your full plan and then determine the implementation plan. Examples of a more long-term focus may include a commitment to having all employees take the Talent and Thinking Style Assessment™. It may be the establishment of a Talent Matrix on all roles in the organization and a commitment to hire using the presented powerful talent-based interview questions. It may be to commit to creating two sculpted job components and three or four performance expectations for each employee by a particular date. It may be your personal commitment to providing successful and recurring performance feedback and to commit to a date when all employees will go through the powerful Career Conversations. Again, the success with this approach is in fully understanding the tools and process and then determining which need to be implemented and when, with an ultimate goal of implementing the entire process.

## Measure and Monitor Your Success

Even though today's management focus is more on emotional connections, successful managers must continue to assess their overall effectiveness based on tangible performance. At no point does the movement to a more humanistic management approach allow for, or accept, less accountability or performance. In fact, this process actually encourages more accountability. Employees are now more responsible to create performance achievement plans. They are more accountable to achieve specific results because you took the time to put them in the right role, set clear expectations, gave them a voice in their work, coached them with performance feedback, and developed customized roles. You invested in each employee. This hard work pays off in the return on this investment – these employees now have every opportunity to perform. It is critical for you to be able to monitor and measure this performance to assess the effectiveness of your management approach.

Not all employees will respond well to this new system of management – particularly if they are not properly matched to their role. If an employee is miscast, despite the effort to place them in the correct role, you will find the miscast employee may have a consistently difficult time performing at the required level. If performance fails, there are several fail-safe measures that will catch the failing performance and allow for corrections so overall performance is not in jeopardy. As performance starts to slip, you will see it as you are more connected to the performance expectations and plans of each employee. Employees create performance plans with empirical expectations and completion dates that hold the employee responsible and accountable for performance. As you review performance plans and watch employee performance on a daily basis, you are now aware of employees who are not performing at expectation. You can immediately intervene with education, coaching, and even role changes in order to ensure the organization's results do not suffer. Because of this, there should be very few opportunities for employees to underperform, unless an employee is truly miscast or is not interested in working. With the Fire Up! Process$^{SM}$ you are now closer to your employees and to the employees' performance. Not only does this create greater employee accountability, but it creates an easier process for you to measure and monitor results.

## Measure the Right Things

This book offers a new and more effective management method that concentrates on the human element and the organization's intellectual capital. Performance expectations were created to define the results employees must contribute – in both performance and empirical results. The connection of performance expectations to financial measurements holds employees accountable for driving results and shows employees the direct connection between their performance and results. Besides showing the connection between performance and results, the metrics now become targets that can be tracked and measured. These empirical targets become the first component of the manager's performance measurement process with employees.

The second component of monitoring and measuring is a review of the engagement level and connectedness of the employee to his/her role. Though the empirical measurements may offer some indication of how fired up the employee is, the real answer will come through a more soft-skill discussion and questioning. This has been established by the Fire Up! tools of setting performance expectations, providing performance feedback, and hosting Career Conversations; each consistently brings you face-to-face with the employee. Dialog, conversation, and discussion are critical in helping you know what the employee feels about his/her role, performance, and impact.

Here are the best ways to assess the emotional connectedness of the employee to his/her role.

- Create a weekly meeting time to review performance plans, assess performance, and discuss obstacles, challenges, and successes.

- Observe performance by becoming more visible and available to employees during their work day.

- Host quarterly surveys to assess employee attitudes about work, performance, and management style. Consider creating your own survey (limit to four to six questions) or use the powerful Gallup Organization's Q12® as presented in *First Break All The Rules* by Marcus Buckingham and Curt Coffman. The more employee-focused the workplace, the more valued and important the employee feels. The more positive responses are made to survey questions such as the Gallup Q12®, the more connected the employee is to his/her environment and manager.

Today's managers monitor and measure performance with both empirical performance targets and by more intangible personal assessments of employee engagement, commitment, and interest levels. Both are measureable to ensure performance is directed to required levels. Though most industrial age managers are capable with the empirical measurements, many are less effective reading employee emotions, interests, and talents. Using the Fire Up! Process<sup>SM</sup> will give you practice with the human side of management, the side that actually drives today's performance.

## Staying Strong

As you have spent time with each employee in his/her daily performance, recurring performance feedback, and discussion of employee development and the future, you have seen the increasing connection of the employee to his/her work and the workplace. So who helps you improve? Who helps you become better at the skills that influence millennial management?

Organizations that implement millennial management implement it at all levels. It is critical your manager host the same discussions, conversations, feedback, and expectations you host with your employees. It is critical you continue your personal development for your intellectual, emotional, and performance benefit. Now that you see the components of performance, start to assess your components: where are you best matched, what skills can be improved, where do you wish to be in one year or three years? As you see the power of both the intellectual and emotional connection with your employees, insist on it from your manager.

## Using the Fire Up Process<sup>SM</sup> to Create the Stand Out Organization

My goal has been to help you create a powerful performing workforce. The best way to create extraordinary customer service is to have extraordinary employees. Only then will employees be committed enough to their roles to provide responses that consistently wow the customer, build their loyalty, and drive your profitability.

Earlier in the text, I introduced the thinking by Dr. John Fleming and Jim Asplund in their book *Human Sigma*. It presented that dissatisfied and satisfied customers buy similar amounts. The great increases in purchases (goods or services) came from loyal customers, not satisfied customers. The difference between satisfied and loyal customers was in the emotional connection the customer had to the brand, product, or organization (employee). Now, consider the caliber of employee you have developed using the Fire Up! Process[SM]. You have searched to find employees who are intellectually connected to their work – they love what they do because it is in line with their talents, values, and interests. You encouraged these talents by creating customized roles through job sculpting and giving each employee a voice in how he/she completes his/her work through performance expectations. You further connected to the employee by spending time with him/her through meaningful feedback and performance development. When done well, you have a very engaged and excited employee. This employee is now very focused on the needs of the customer because you are very focused on the needs of the employee. If the employee felt that his/her needs in the workplace were not met, he/she would be distracted away from the need to respond to customers in a stand out way. But since he/she is well respected, is clear about his/her role, likes what he/she does, has a good relationship with you, and sees a clear path for the future, he/she can direct his/her efforts towards the customer.

Organizations that provide stand out service follow the Humanetrics' Loyalty Formula; it has two critical components:

1. Every service event must *get it right* for the customer (the employee must know what the customer needs and provide it as needed each time), and

2. Every service event must *do something more* to get the attention of the customer and leave a powerful impression.

Or think of it this way:

1. When you don't get it right for a customer, you create a dissatisfied customer – the customer is unlikely to come back and will share the negative experience with his/her friends.

2. When you get it right for a customer (part 1 of the Loyalty Formula), you create a satisfied customer – the customer may or may not come back.

3. When you get it right and do something more (parts 1 and 2 of the Loyalty Formula), you create a loyal customer – the customer will come back and share the positive experience with his/her friends.

This means your employees have nearly complete control in creating dissatisfied, satisfied, or loyal customers. Your employees have the ability of creating a stand out organization or an average one. Employees who are miscast in the wrong roles, and are not supported and developed in the workplace, are unable to consistently provide the basic expectations of a customer; you, therefore, create dissatisfied customers. This can destroy your business. Employees who may be in the right roles but are not excited and engaged in what they do (they do just enough not to be fired) may occasionally satisfy a customer, but a satisfied customer does not always return. Again, your business suffers. Employees, who are well hired in the right role, have connected intellectually to their work and emotionally to you, approach their work with greater effort and energy. This is visible to customers as the employee invents more significant responses, takes greater service risks to provide service in an unforgettable and loyalty building way, and connects personally to customers. These employees are the power in your service workplace. These employees drive performance and achieve results. These employees commit when others do not. This commitment is because of the steps of the Fire Up! Process$^{SM}$. It has a direct ability to create a stand out workplace that provides consistently extraordinary customer service.

When you slept last night, the world changed. The departure of the industrial age ushered in a new and significantly different intellectual, service, and innovation age. Employees, what they know and how they feel, now influence performance. Feelings, emotions, passions, and interests now connect employees to their roles or disconnect them if they are not addressed. Managers are now, more than ever, the guiding force in all performance. A new economy has demanded a new form of management.

Managers must always develop a management style based on the needs of their employees. Today's employees need nurturing, communication, collaboration, and connection. Today's employees no longer respond to demands, dictates, or decisions that do not include them. Today's employees represent the intellectual capital of all organizations; to access this powerful capital, an employee must be intellectually and emotionally connected to his/her role and emotionally connected to you, the manager. Create this connection and they perform. Fail to create it and they do as little as possible at work, until they decide to leave. Your organization and your customers feel these effects.

Today is the day to recommit to the intellectual power of your employees. Review the Fire Up! Process[SM] and build a powerful action plan to implement its steps. People quit people before they quit companies. Don't encourage your employees to quit you. Do the right things for your employees; they will become loyal, and influence your customers to be loyal as well. Fire Up! your employees and they will smoke your competition.

# Bibliography and Resources for More Information

Barner, Robert Ph.D., *Bench Strength*, New York: Amacom, 2006.

Buckingham, Marcus and Curt Coffman, *First, Break All of the Rules*, New York: Simon and Schuster, 1999.

Buckingham, Marcus and Donald Clifton, *Next, Discover your Strengths*, Simon and Schuster, New York, 2001.

Coughlin, Linda, Ellen Wingard, and Keith Hollihan, eds, *Enlightened Power, How Women Are Transforming the Practice of Leadership*, New York: Jossey-Bass, 2005.

Dauten, Dale, *The Gifted Boss*, New York: William Morrow and Company, 1999.

Fleming, John H. Ph.D. and Jim Asplund, *Human Sigma*, New York: Gallup Press, 2007.

Frankel, Dr. Lois P., *See Jane Lead*, New York: Warner Business Books, 2007.

Freiberg, Kevin and Jackie, *Boom! 7 Choices for Blowing the Doors off Business-as-Usual*, Nashville: Thomas Nelson, 2007.

Fritz, Roger, *Think Like A Manager*, Shawnee Mission, KS: National Seminars Publication, 1994.

Godin, Seth, Editor, *The Big Moo*, New York: Portfolio (the Penguin Group), 2005.

Hartman, Dr. Taylor, *The People Code*, New York: Scribner, 2007.

Hathaway, Patti, *Giving and Receiving Feedback*, Menlo Park, CA: Crisp Publications, 1998.

Heath, Chip and Dan Heath, *Made to Stick*, New York: Random House, 2007.

Helgesen, Sally, *The Female Advantage*, New York: Currency (Doubleday), 1990.

Hermane, Roger E. and Joyce L.Gioia, *How to Become an Employer of Choice*, Winchester, VA: Oakhill Press, 2000.

Kline, Nancy, *Time to Think*, London: Cassell Illustrated (Octopus Publishing Group Ltd.), 1999.

Muchnick, Marc, *Naked Management*, Boca Raton, FL: St. Lucie Press, 1996.

Patterson, Kerry, Joseph Grenny, Ron McMillan, and Al Switzler. *Crucial Conversations: Tools for Talking When Stakes are High*. New York: McGraw-Hill, 2002.

Pfau, Bruce N. Ph.D. and Ira T.Kay, Ph.D., *The Human Capital Edge*, New York: McGraw Hill, 2002.

Rath, Tom, *Strengthsfinder 2.0*, New York: Gallup Press, 2007.

Robinson, Dana Gaines and James C. Robinson, *Performance Consulting: A Practical Guide for HR and Learning Professionals*, San Francisco: Berrett-Koehler Publishers, 2008.

Sartain, Libby and Mark Schumann, *Brand from the Inside*, New York: Jossey-Bass, 2006.

Sirota, David, Louis Mischkind, and Michael Irwin Meltzer, *The Enthusiastic Employee*, Upper Saddle River, NJ: Wharton School Publishing, 2005.

Stallard, Michael Lee, *Fired Up or Burned Out*, Nashville: Thomas Nelson, 2007.

Tulgan, Bruce, *Recruiting the Workforce of the Future*, Amherst, MA: HRD Press, 2000.

Want, Jerome, *Corporate Culture: Illuminating the Black Hole*, New York: St Martin's Press, 2006.

## About the Author

Jay Forte is a powerful performance speaker, consultant, talent strategist, and author. Originally trained as a CPA, nationally ranked Thought Leader, and founder/president of Humanetrics, Jay has more than twenty years of teaching managers and leaders how to Fire Up! their employees to maximize performance and results.

A specialist in employee engagement, high performance workplaces, and advancing the role of women in management, Jay has worked with companies to successfully change their approach to attracting, hiring, developing, and retaining the best employees. He has been widely published in the areas of millennial management, employee performance, mentoring, strategy, customer service, and STAND OUT living. He has been interviewed by national publications and is a repeat guest on numerous business talk radio programs for his practical and high-impact solutions to today's intellectual-age workplace challenges.

He is a member of the ASTD (American Society of Training and Development), SHRM (Society of Human Resource Management), ISPI (International Society of Performance Improvement), NSA (National Speakers Association), and the FSA (Florida Speakers Association).

See his practical performance tips blog, titled "BLOGucation," updated daily at www.humanetricsllc.com.